# GENERATIONAL FUSION

*How to Master the Multi-Gen Workforce: Uniting Strengths Across Ages*



NIKHIL RAVAL

Generational Fusion



All information, techniques, ideas and concepts contained within this publication are of the nature of general comment only and are not in any way recommended as individual advice. The intent is to offer a variety of information to provide a wider range of choices now and in the future, recognizing that we all have widely diverse circumstances and viewpoints. Should any reader choose to make use of the information contained herein, this is their decision, and the contributors (and their companies), authors and publishers do not assume any responsibilities whatsoever under any condition or circumstances. It is recommended that the reader obtain their own independent advice.

ISBN:



Published by Happy Self Publishing
www.happyselfpublishing.com
writetous@happyselfpublishing.com

HAPPY
SELF PUBLISHING

# PRAISE FOR THE BOOK

'Nikhil has been deep into exploring the key attributes of this multi-generation workforce and building this insight to see how we best leverage the strength of each. There are a few key attributes which remain constant too across generations, but being aware of intrinsic and extrinsic motivation factors always will help create an ecosystem where every generation thrives.'

**SAMBIT DASH, MD and Country Head (ComputaCenter, India)**

'Nikhil's work brings about some very pertinent nuances to multi-generational diversity. Real-time examples from the corporate world coupled with personal anecdotes offer a perfect balance to your reading experience. A must-read if you are keen to crack the code on "Points of differences" and "Points of parity" in a multi-generational ecosystem.'

**AMARPREET KAUR AHUJA, Chief Human Resources Officer (AstraZeneca, India)**

'*Generational Fusion* on a long flight. Despite being tired, I was immediately pulled in and could not stop. Through a variety of engaging stories, Nikhil takes a very refreshing and practical look at the challenges of managing today's multi-generational workplaces. Not only does he provide deep insights into what drives different generations (from Gen Z to Boomers) but most importantly, he provides concrete and practical advice on how we can bridge generational conflict and turn it into an organizational strength. He beautifully highlights the power and importance of curiosity to foster understanding and create an inclusive workspace where we can all thrive.'

**MELANIE MARTINELLI, CEO, Institute of Transfer Effectiveness (Basel, Switzerland)**

'Nikhil wrestles with a critical topic for all organizations and societies that want to perform well in the long-term: How do you get different people with different personalities, from different generations, to live and work together to maximize the strengths of everyone? And comes up with some useful and practical insights for all of us.'

**ALEX HILL, Thinkers Top 50 Leaders,**
**Author of *Centennials* (London, UK)**

'In an era marked by intense polarization, Nikhil's insights on fostering multi-generational harmony in the workplace are a much-needed breath of fresh air. His ability to simplify such a complex subject is truly impressive. With practical toolkits and real-world examples drawn from his own extensive experience, his book serves as an invaluable resource for any business leader or manager looking to harness the power of each generation.'

**DR. SANDHYA KARPE, Human Capital Ctr Leader,**
**Program Dir, DE&I Conference Board (Singapore)**

'Not many people have done such deep and meaningful work understanding a problem that has been a part of humanity since its very existence. Nikhil's book is a practical guide for practitioners to implement practices that promote inter-generational inclusion. Something that can benefit us all greatly both personally and professionally.'

**RICHA SINGH, VP HR - L&D, Diversity Equity & Inclusion**
**(Axis Max Life Insurance, India)**

'A key challenge encountered by business and CXO leaders is the ability to get work done by a disparate group of employees, varying in age, qualifications, as well as predispositions. COVID has further exacerbated this challenge, opening the door of working from home. If you need a cheat code for this complicated riddle, your answer lies here. Nikhil's book talks to you about bringing forth the daily challenges that managers face and tries to provide solutions from leading organizations' practices. In a small book, he has brought a roomful of wisdom.'

**MURTHY CHAGANTI, MD & CEO, Asianet Satellite (India), Ex-CEO Airtel Tigo (Ghana)**

'A Multi-Generational workforce is a reality today. The success of how we manage this will really determine the success of the organization. How can Boomers and Xers understand the career expectations and values of Gen Y and Z? How can iGen tap the experience of the older generations? Nikhil captures all the key aspects of how to make a Multi-Gen workforce unleash its potential. He looks at the key elements of values, communication, ageism, hybrid and others which impact a Multi-Gen workplace. A must-read for all managers to succeed in today's professional world.'

**ROB NIKKEL, CEO, Intranet Connections (Vancouver, Canada)**

'In *Generational Fusion,* author Nikhil takes a refreshing and practical look at the challenges of managing today's multi-generational workplaces. Through engaging stories and sharp insights, he explores how generational differences can become surprising strengths when approached with the right mindset. At the heart of bridging generational conflicts in the workplace is curiosity—a powerful tool that fosters understanding, adaptability, and collaboration, turning those challenges into opportunities for innovation and shared success. This book is a must-have for leaders ready to embrace the complexities of building stronger, more connected teams.'

**DR. DIANE HAMILTON, Syndicated National Radio Host, Author of *Curiosity Unleashed* (Phoenix, USA)**

'This book comes at a time when the Multi-Gen workforce is a reality. Most organizations are grappling with how to keep all generations motivated and engaged. With sharp insights and real-world examples, Nikhil breaks down and brings a fresh perspective on what drives each generation and how leaders and employees at all levels can leverage the strengths of each generation. A brilliant read for all HR, L&D and Business Leaders who lead or manage a multi gen team.'

**DR. MANAVI PATHAK, PhD, Head L & D, Samsung R&D Institute of India**

'In a world where four generations coexist in the workplace, Nikhil offers a timely and practical guide to navigating the complexities of multi-generational dynamics. Building on the Gen Z-focused foundation of his first book, Nikhil broadens the lens to examine the unique perspectives, tensions, and opportunities that arise when Boomers, Gen X, Millennials, and Gen Z share the same workspace. He explores how changing workplaces, evolving worker roles, and shifting work paradigms impact collaboration and engagement across generations through compelling client stories, actionable insights, and practical tools. From addressing hybrid work challenges to bridging communication gaps, this book provides a clear roadmap to transform generational differences into strengths.

**STEPHEN KREMPL, Ex CLO Starbucks, Author of *The 5% Zone: Visibility Strategies that Get you Recognized and Rewarded in Any Organization* (Nashville, USA)**

'This comprehensive book is a must for all budding handlers of people. The family was the bedrock of development. For many, it still is, but a world of fast communications, international dealings, express travel and rapid technological development exerts strains on the traditional sequences of life in a way that demands greater understanding and more skilful training. Nikhil has explained this in a lucid and illuminating way, pointing to the opportunities and potential pitfalls of a rapidly developing society. As he rightly tells us, "Work" is a changing concept. So, of course, is "Value." The annihilation of copyright and the demise of all but the most creative jobs by AI is bringing a change of tsunami proportions to who we are. Indeed, we are being told we must now define who we want to be for the first time in human history when it is possible to activate the answer. Nikhil is to be thanked for showing us the path we are inexorably on. He will be in a strong position to help us over the boulders and rocks of tomorrow's world.

**SIR JOHN BITTLESTON (Singapore)**

'*Generational Fusion* is a must-read for anyone navigating today's diverse workplace. With sharp insights drawn from years of consulting, Nikhil skilfully unpacks the complexities of managing multiple generations—from Gen Z to Boomers—and offers practical strategies for turning generational differences into organizational strengths. This book doesn't just identify the challenges; it provides actionable solutions for fostering collaboration, empathy, and innovation across the workforce. A powerful guide for leaders looking to thrive in a post-pandemic world!'

**TESS BRIGHAM, MFT, Columnist: *CNBC, Forbes,* featured in *NYTimes, SF Chronicle, Oprah Magazine***

## BONUS GIVEAWAY 1

SCAN ME

Discover ten powerful leadership models designed to help you navigate and manage generational diversity in the workplace. From adaptive leadership to coaching and transformational styles, these models offer practical strategies to foster collaboration, enhance engagement, and drive results across all age groups.

## BONUS GIVEAWAY 2

SCAN ME

Lead with confidence using seven proven leadership frameworks tailored for a diverse, multi-generational team. These frameworks provide practical strategies to bridge generational differences, foster collaboration, and drive high performance in today's evolving workplace.

## BONUS GIVEAWAY 3

SCAN ME

Navigate the complexities of a multi-generational workforce with this practical, step-by-step workbook. Filled with exercises, real-world case studies, and actionable insights, this resource will help you develop leadership strategies that foster collaboration, engagement, communication, and productivity performance across all age groups.

Bridging Generations: A Practical Workbook for Multi-Gen Collaboration

## BONUS GIVEAWAY 4

SCAN ME

Test your leadership approach with this interactive quiz to uncover insights into communication styles, workplace motivation, feedback and performance reviews, leadership management styles, and technology adoption across generations. Gain a deeper understanding of how to bridge generational gaps and enhance team collaboration with targeted strategies.

*To my mother, who was the purest, gentlest soul on earth. Her unwavering love and wisdom of spreading goodness to everyone was the greatest gift to my brother and me.*

*To all mothers who give a lifetime of sacrifices in building the next generation.*

# *Table of Content*

## Your Generational Tool Kit

# INTRODUCTION:

In 2021, I wrote my first book, *Target Gen Z – Understanding the Gen Z Mindset on Brands, Work Life, Learning and More*. The book talks about the hopes and aspirations of the newest generation entering the workforce and various workplace dimensions and their impact on them. I have tried to distil my observations from client stories and learnings from my 12 years of high-end leadership consulting work on how companies grapple with talent issues, especially attracting, retaining and engaging Gen Z.

This writing was my first maiden attempt at a full-length book, but my knowledge of this generation actually deepened quite substantially only when clients started to ask me to design workshops and deliver talks on Gen Z and their work-related issues in their organizations. It was time to put some of the research and what I saw in my consulting work back into practice. The range of topics for these workshops would include everything from giving leaders a high-level orientation of who this new generation was to understanding their workplace preferences in an ever-changing context. For example, how do we upskill an incoming Gen Z cohort with the debate of AI taking away many entry-level jobs? Or what should the employers do when it comes to defining the office place rules? Should it be all Remote versus All at Office versus Hybrid? Key considerations include the critical role of mental well-being in a post-COVID world, the growing emphasis on Diversity and Inclusion highlighted by movements like Black Lives Matter and #MeToo, and the urgent need for sustainability in the face of overwhelming evidence of shifting climate patterns and an impending energy crisis.

Despite trepidations about how the book of a first-time author would be accepted, the sales of the book have grown steadily, having now sold in over 30 countries, with the US and India being the top two markets. This, in turn, led to my second invitation for a Ted Talk where the focus was to motivate Gen Zs. All the learnings about the 'iGen' were like peeling an onion; there were more layers, and each layer brought more questions and taught me new things.

This was also when I launched my first podcast, *Working with Gen Z*. The podcast became a gateway to bringing the next level of insights to understanding Gen Z. I brought global experts in all different fields ranging from financial planners to entrepreneurs, relationship experts to cyber security professionals, AI to creativity, inter culture to sustainability experts, each trying to shed light on their respective topics in the context of Gen Z. We explored the various dimensions of these topics, delving into Gen Z's perspectives, their reactions, and the most effective ways to navigate and address these issues. Each episode ultimately gave a crisp Call-2-Action and suggestions with clear dos and don'ts for the managers leading them and the Gen Z's themselves. Launching this niche podcast gave everyone from the HR fraternity to academia to clients the view beneath the iceberg and a far more holistic side of this generation. The podcast is now heard in over 60 countries, with US, and India as the top two locations. But the icing on the cake was when the podcast was rated among the Top 5 Gen Z podcasts in the world, over 250 Gen Z podcasts today. (See details in the i-Gen Hub).

## Why a second book on Multi Generations and not a sequel to Gen Z, you may ask?

As I did more client work, it was clear leaders managing Gen Z continued to show curiosity in understanding them better. However, all my conversations with such managers revealed only one side of the story. In many of my diagnostic meetings with Gen Zs reporting to bosses from Gen Y or Gen X and hearing their perspectives of their bosses, it was becoming clear that the Gen Zs shared their own 'lens' of how they saw bosses. They believed it wasn't always just 'them' who were the problem. Tensions were seen among Gen Y managers managing Gen Zs, and Millennials were also complaining about bosses from Generation Xers. There were also Boomers in many organizations adding to the complexity of four generations in the organizations. So, what were the real sources of conflicts among the generations? It was everything that seems to have changed – the **Workplace, the Worker and the Work** itself in a post-COVID world. Here is a sneak peek of what was brewing

**Workplace**: When I talk about changing **the workplace**, I refer to the obvious or subtle differences that came with what 'hybrid' meant for everyone. I saw companies try everything from what was the 'At-Will' Model to 'The Split Week Model' to 'Shift Work to the Week-by-Week' model. Each worker in the system had a say based on what suited them the most, which made some happy but also many unhappy. These decisions had an obvious effect on things like the level of collaboration that existed or didn't exist between teams. It also posed questions on how employees will serve clients remotely. What is the best way to communicate with them? What will be a good way to collaborate across the organization, both internally and externally? Will it impact productivity or increase it? Also, in many instances, contrary to the common view that the older generations would have preferred coming to the office, they were actually adjusting nicely to working from home, but it was the younger generations who were feeling increasingly lonely and wanted to come to the office. Also, if you had a hybrid way of working, what should be the timings for a flexible work schedule? Should employees be expected to be connected late in the evenings, given the flexibility to work? Can they take on new work in their spare time? How would young employees experience the culture of the firm and meet clients working from home and so on? Should companies continue to invest in physical offices going forward, or should they invest in technologies that allow for better virtual collaboration? Was some form of hybrid becoming the 'new norm'?

**Worker**: When I talk about **'worker'** the one phenomenon which has been happening is the increase in the average life expectancy of people around the world. It is inching from the late 60s in many parts of the world and is predicted to touch the late 80s in many others. This also meant employees had more time on hand from the traditionally defined age of retirement of 60-65 years. However, external factors, such as the ongoing conflicts among nations, led to a recession in many parts of the world. Demand and consumption were shrinking, putting companies under a lot of stress to perform and meet street expectations often leading to attrition and layoffs. All of this was taking a mental toll, and the added burden of saving finances for themselves and their families forced employees from Boomers and Xers to extend their work runway leading to a redefined retirement work age. But this too had its consequences. By staying longer, were the experienced generations blocking the way for more meaningful roles for the younger generations in the system? Would Boomers or Xers be overlooked for additional development and neglected for promotions? Was career spillover a crisis or opportunity for firms? How serious was the issue of mental well-being among employees? What leadership skills would be needed if a younger manager led an older employee? Would lack of development lead to more attrition and lower engagement?

**Work**: Finally, when I talk about **'work'** itself changing: With the onslaught of new technologies of AI, Machine Learning, Cloud, and Data Analytics, the nature of work itself was changing drastically. Companies were seriously mulling over things like: How many entry-level jobs (in many industries, especially in those like manufacturing) would really be done by humans in the coming years? What percentage of a business can be automated? How should companies look at hiring young employees? Will it be based on degrees or skills? How do companies help the more experienced employees to be more 'Learning Agile' (i.e. to unlearn old ways of doing business) and to adapt to newer business models? Should the younger generations like Gen Z feel more confident due to their familiarity with technology? Should the older generation be more nervous if they do not adapt to it? Was the emergence of new technology creating a sense of insecurity or friction among employees at different levels? For all generations in the post-COVID world, how much of the work was done for money versus something that was creating value? The old paradigm of 'you give me time and I give you money' was shifting to 'Value Exchange' between employee and employer. What value do I bring to the employer, and also, what value does my employer offer me? Work had to have

> The old paradigm of 'you give me time and I give you money' was shifting to 'Value Exchange' between employee and employer. What value do I bring to the employer, and also, what value does my employer offer me? Work had to have relevance and, therefore, **'meaning was becoming the new money.'**

relevance and, therefore, **'meaning was becoming the new money.'**

So, all of this had the makings of a perfect storm but it seemed like the tip of the iceberg. Every employee from each generation brought their own preference to this changing workplace, worker and nature of work. After more than two decades of full-time work and now in my capacity as a free-lance gig worker, I try to picture myself as a manager or sub-ordinate in many situations I saw my clients in and realized that the generational differences were quite real. When not addressed adequately, it caused conflict, created a lack of en-gagement, and resulted in low morale and higher attrition.

So, was there an antidote to this? But the more I reflected, I also realized Multi Generations have always existed in other parts of our lives. We see generational play in families. Busi-nesses have run with Multi Generations; in politics, we've seen leaders from different generations leading nations; in education, the experienced generation teaches the younger generation; in sports, coach-coachee relationships have al-ways existed showcasing generational gap, and so is the case often amongst our friends as well. With enough test of time, it seems generational gaps and relations have worked over centuries.

But, perhaps the most visible place of experience for gener-ations would be for those who are parents. Every parent can vouch for their own share of some 'tenuous' phases of raising children, just as the children would have to recount their 'own' moments from their perspective. However, every parent we know who has raised good children needs a collective effort to achieve success. There was a healthy appreciation of relationships on both sides as kids went from becoming teenagers to adults and as parents went from working parents and fulfilling their duties to attaining retirement and then ageing.

But beyond the general parenting analogy, there was an immediate personal context. The Gen Zs in our house will enter the workforce soon, and what will that experience look like for them? Both my boys had done internships already, forming their views of what they would want and not want from bosses. I also thought: What if I were working full time, and how would I have handled some of the changing workplace contexts? What will be my sons' and nephew's expectations from their employers? Or, in their case, if they wished to become entrepreneurs, how would they manage older generations in their ventures?

With the changing workplace context, appreciating the other perspective seems obvious and evident, yet it seems easier said than done. So, what comes in our way? Is it the biases of our own lens? Are we hard-wired so strongly that it is the inability to let go of our way of doing things? Does a new approach become an opportunity for learning for each generation or a reason for conflict? Well, maybe a bit of both.

This book attempts to help leaders see and lay out the Multi-Gen landscape so that managers can appreciate the various points of difference that can prop up. But equally how we can leverage the differences and turn them into strengths towards a unified, collective and collaborative workplace. Often in life, as in business, we need to step out of the trenches to see the forest from the trees. I hope the external lens I get as a consultant brings some insights into the changing workplace demographics. It will be far from perfect, but together we can learn and improvise. As you read through this, please share your stories and insights (as you have done for my first book) so we can bring new ways of managing the Multi-Gen Workforce. The power of 'we' in generations always trumps the power of 'I' as an individual.

Enjoy the reading and join me on this journey to transform multi-generational challenges into opportunities for growth and success.

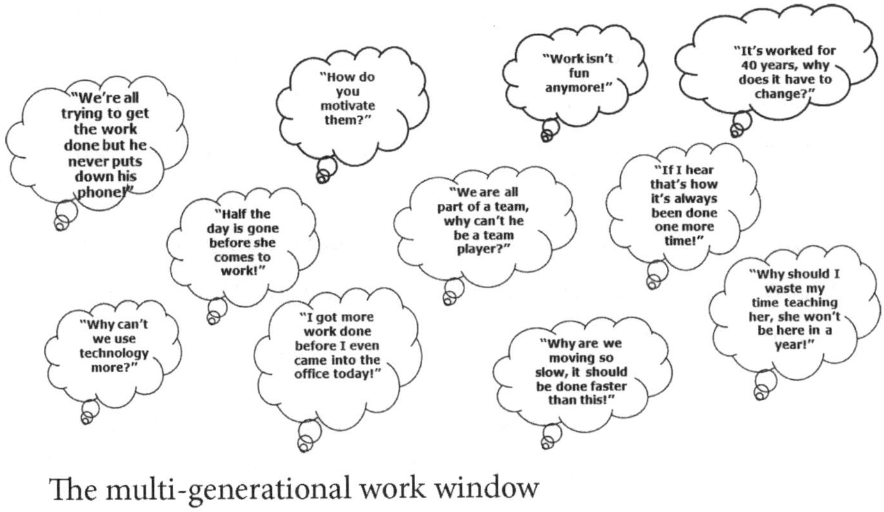


The multi-generational work window

## Structure of Book

The book is structured as a practitioner's guide, designed to provide actionable insights for managing a multi-generational workforce. To that extent, I have tried to keep the language simple and lucid. The general flow of each chapter will feature a topic of discussion which will have either a client or personal story, a detailed explanation of the concept on hand, and finally, some practical solutions to the theme being discussed.

The client stories are there to provide real-world examples and context, concept explanations break down essential theories and principles, solutions offer practical advice and methods for application, and in some chapters, some fun quizzes are introduced to reinforce understanding and retention of the material.

**Part One** delves into what I call the **Points of Differences (PODs)** within a Multi-Gen workforce. This section aims to provide readers with a deep understanding of each generation's unique characteristics and challenges. Here, I examine the varying communication styles, emerging workplace trends and generational preferences, work habits, values and technological proficiencies that can influence team dynamics and productivity.

**Part Two** shifts the focus to bridging these differences through **Points of Parity (POPs).** It offers strategies and practices to create a more cohesive and collaborative work environment by leveraging commonalities and fostering mutual respect.

The final section of the book is your **Generational Toolkit**. In this, you will find a few short cases that describe the typical generational challenges you may have seen in your organization. You can use these to facilitate discussions internally or in your own workshops. Additionally, there are cheat sheets that can be used for your presentations. Finally, there are some quizzes in select chapters and glossaries to help you and your colleagues in enhancing generational vocabulary and knowledge.

**How to Read**: While the two sections are independent, it is recommended you read in sequence (Part One, followed by Two) so you understand the differences of a Multi-Gen workforce first, and then it logically builds in helping you understand ways to bridge those challenges. Within each section, you can read any chapter as it is written to be standalone. Below is a short description of each chapter.

## Section 1 (PODs – Points of Differences)

Chapter 1: **Value Paradox:** Understanding key generational values and the potential clashes it can bring at the workplace. How generational values influence workplace dynamics, collaboration, benefits, culture and other dimensions.

Chapter 2: **Hybrid Realities and Office-Hybrid Evolution:** We explore how the traditional office model has evolved into flexible hybrid frameworks driven by changing workforce expectations and technological advancements. It delves into the shifts across generations, highlighting how each group navigates the transition from in-office routines to blended work environments.

Chapter 3: **Generations and Communication:** What are the different preferred communication styles of generations highlighting the need for formality, technology and feedback. The chapter offers insights into bridging differences to foster collaboration and understanding.

Chapter 4: **Ageism @Workplace:** What is Ageism? What pervasive biases and stereotypes affect both younger and older generations in the workplace? What's the impact, and how do we combat Ageism?

## Section 2 (POPs – Points of Parity)

---

Chapter 5: **Biases-Stereotypes and Meta-Stereotypes:** This chapter delves into the impact of unconscious biases on perceptions, the role of stereotypes in creating generational divides, and the influence of meta-stereotypes—how individuals believe others perceive their generation—on communication, collaboration, and trust. It also offers practical strategies to recognize and overcome these challenges.

Chapter 6: **Generational Context:** The chapter talks about understanding how historical events, cultural shifts, and technological advancements shape the values, behaviors, and expectations of different generations. By understanding these influences, we can better interpret their actions and bridge workplace gaps effectively. Three specific practices are shared to overcome generational biases and stereotypes.

Chapter 7: **Career Spillovers:** This chapter talks about the impact of career spillovers on generations. If carefully designed it can help both younger and experienced generations create a collaborative environment which drives mutual learning and benefits.

Chapter 8: **Shadow Boards:** The chapter explores understanding what are Shadow Boards, their benefits and downsides. How do companies form and implement them? Examples are shared of firms that have successfully created Shadow Boards.

## Generational Tool Kit

**Case Scenarios:** This section features brief scenarios showcasing challenges in a multi-generational workforce, encouraging readers to analyze and propose their own solutions.

**Generational Cheat Sheet:** The Generational Cheat Sheet offers facts, key insights, and a glossary to enhance your workshops on multi-generational dynamics.

**Understanding i-Gen** is your go-to resource for all things Gen Z. You can get more information on understanding Gen Z through my book, podcast, YouTube channel and speaking engagements.

# PART I:

## Understanding the (PODs): Points of Differences of the Multi-Generational Workforce: The Changing Workplace, Worker and Work

CHAPTER 1

# The Value Paradox: Understanding Shared and Divergent Values across Generations

'Your beliefs become your thoughts, your thoughts become your words, your words become your actions, your actions become your habits, your habits become your values, your values become your destiny.'

– *Mahatma Gandhi*

## Client Story

In many of the client workshops that I do, I have often used an activity called the **'River of Life.'** It is an activity where participants reflect on the pivotal movements of their lives right from childhood to their current age. The purpose is to recall the key milestones and the leadership lessons they learned. Who was instrumental in giving them that lesson? From this, they have to write a short definition of what leadership means to them. It is called the River of Life because our lives are like a river, which often goes through ups and downs from mountains to valleys and plains, sometimes slow and fast. The second part of this exercise also involves thinking about what they want the river to look like going forward.

So, as people do this exercise, we see them draw their 'rivers' when they were teenagers. It could be a teacher who changed their life in how they approached a particular subject; for example, Math, making it so easy and interesting that their fear of Math was gone. Or a parent, uncle/aunt or sibling who taught them the importance of life skills like hard work, honesty, punctuality, and discipline. For many others, it could be their first travel overseas and learnings from it, a good boss they've had or a bad boss or even their children who have taught them the life lesson of being 'helpful, living in the present and being happy.' For the second part of the River, many have a directional clarity, but many have not thought through how they wish to see the remaining 20-30-40 years ahead of them, both professionally or personally. How do they want to be remembered at work upon retirement? How do they want to be remembered at home among their family members?

**Value Lessons**: It is quite a reflective exercise. For many, it is hard to recollect life events. It makes for a very emotive scene for most. Upon completion, participants often confess they have not thanked some key people who have shaped them enough. Some of their greatest learnings of life or values have often come from someone younger than them, without a PhD., without a big designation or who did without the official hierarchical reporting relationship at work. These lessons or values have stayed with them forever, turning them into who they are now.

From the exercise, we try to draw upon these few things:

**First**: Definition of leadership – Making people realize that it is much beyond a title, salary, degree, position or hierarchy. It can come from any walk of life and carries on who you are beyond the corner office or the professional title. You could be a good boss, but if you are not a good father, son or spouse, how good of a leader are you? How you lead can often have an impact on someone older than you.

**Second**: Where do you feel the River is going? What do you want it to look like in the years to come?

**Third**: When we start thinking about what lies ahead of us, we have to realize that we have a limited runway on the impact we can make on others in our lives, whether at work, with friends or at home. These lessons of leadership are almost always shaped by none other than our values.

When we start thinking about what lies ahead of us, we have to realize that we have a limited runway on the impact we can make on others in our lives, whether at work, with friends or at home. These lessons of leadership are almost always shaped by none other than our values.

**Fourth**: What are you doing today so YOU can show up as a leader on someone's 'River' (i.e. a younger employee mentioning your name for a value they learned from you)?

> What are you doing today so YOU can show up as a leader on someone's 'River' (i.e. a younger employee mentioning your name for a value they learned from you)?

These third and fourth questions often always stump people. They need to deeply reflect on their purpose or goal and, more importantly, what values they stand for and how many people they have impacted.

In this chapter, we will explore the values of a few key areas for each generation and discuss the different values, opportunities, or sources of conflict among generations. It is the basis on which subsequent chapters are written, and where the generations see and bring different values. In the second half of the book (or Chapter 6) we will go into detail about the historical context that has shaped the values of each generation and how we can overcome the biases and stereotypes that may have been hardwired into us.

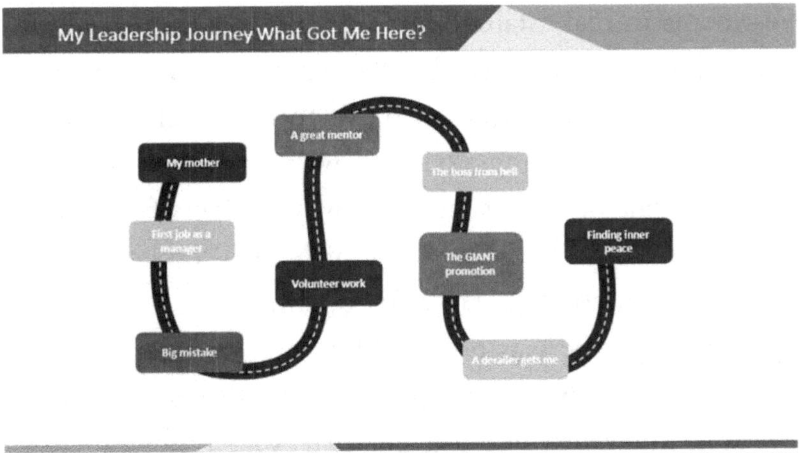


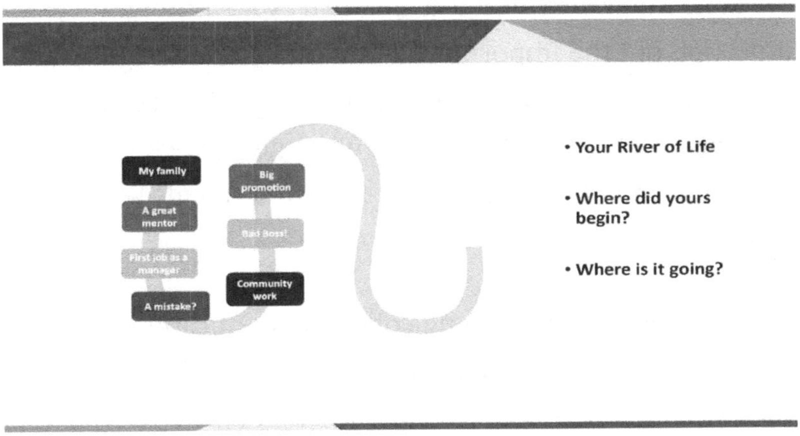


## Money

### Client Story

In my first year as a financial planner with a large financial advisory firm in 1995, I had a range of clients I worked with, but two client stories always stood out distinctly. My first client was an elderly couple whose net worth was about $10 million. Much of this wealth was accumulated through investments in real estate. John had built this throughout his life by buying several small apartments which he rented out to students in the college town of Lansing, Michigan. Upon visiting us and seeking advice on what to do with his portfolio, our one obvious suggestion was to diversify by asking him if he would liquidate some of his real estate holdings and invest in equities. He refused, simply because equities are something he was not familiar with, and he felt it was okay for him to build his nest primarily through real estate. What he knew very well was that real estate is not a very liquid asset, but the importance of building a nest egg is something he needed to start building at a young age. His children were also well off, and he would ultimately give his property to a trust and allow the income from the rentals to fund his charity.

In the second story, a young college student came to us with her boyfriend because she had inherited $500K from her father, who'd passed away. Knowing her story, we advised that it was a perfect opportunity for her to invest the money into something good and stable, which could help her with her life goals as the money appreciated. She said she would think about it and never came back. About six months later, she returned saying she had $25K to invest and asked where we should put it. When we inquired about the remainder of the inheritance money, she said it was all 'gone.' In the past six months, she splurged that money by taking trips to Florida, and Europe, including paying for friends, buying expensive items like jet skis, and emptying all the inheritance money in just four months. If it was invested even in safe (non-risky) assets, this money could have served her as a stream of income through her 20s, 30s and onwards.

Most stories about the values of generations (like the two above) are anecdotal, which means our own experience determines either a positive or a negative message for older and younger generations. So, when it comes to attitudes towards saving money, there are plenty of assumptions people can make about them. As we apply a generational lens to the money each generation handles, we see that it is in different ways. After all, people have grown up in different eras and place value on different commodities. Some are busy saving for retirement while others are squirreling away their pennies in order to see the world one day. Let us look at briefly how each generation sees money. Do note that the context of where you are could be different, so the nuances highlight that generational money behaviors are shaped as much by local realities as by shared global trends.

**Silent Generation** (1928-1945): This generation often views money as a hard-earned asset, associating it with security and stability. Having experienced economic hardships like the Great Depression or its aftermath, they value savings, frugality, and a conservative approach to spending. Money represents a form of safety net that ensures their future.

**Baby Boomers** (born 1946-1964): Baby Boomers often have a lot to say about the younger generations, but in reality, the financial landscape has traditionally been more in their favor than it has for any generation after them. They are generally referred to as the 'wealthiest generation.' People in this generation have been good at saving, but not necessarily because they've had to be; more likely because they just can. Many grew up during economic booms and see financial growth as a path to independence and a comfortable retirement. Their approach often emphasizes investment in assets, particularly real estate, and creating a legacy for their families. They are a generation who inherited a frugal attitude from their parents' generation, who lived through rationing.

**Generation X** (born 1965-1980): Sometimes known as the 'forgotten generation.' Generally, they've seen more financial strife than the Boomers before them, but this doesn't put them off spending! Gen Xers typically view money as a means to balance security and enjoyment. With a tendency toward skepticism due to economic recessions and shifts, they prioritize financial independence, cautious investment, and work-life balance, often seeking to provide stability for their families while also enjoying the present. On top of this, many of them are splitting the funds that they have saved between caring for their elderly parents and supporting their 'zellenial' children, who are likely to return to live at home at some point during their mid-twenties.

**Millennials** (born 1981-1996): For Millennials, money often represents freedom and experiences. This generation tends to prioritize spending on experiences over possessions and values flexibility, whether that means working freelance, traveling, or pursuing personal passions. The 2008 financial crash hit the older group within this generation, while younger Millennials faced extortionate university costs and difficulty breaking into the job market. Despite this, Millennials are the generation that is most comfortable with making short-term sacrifices in order to save for future experiences. They also view money as a tool for making a difference and valuing social and environmental investments.

**Generation Z** (born 1997-2012): Finally, we reach Generation Z, a group of savvy digital natives. Unsurprisingly, there are many similarities between Gen Z and Millennials in saving attitudes. This is largely due to their aptitude for technology and their preference for mobile banking. Most Gen Z savers check their bank balance at least once a day and are likely to use savvy banking apps that allow them to move their money around between their accounts and know exactly how much they are managing to save. Like older generations, Gen Z still enjoys treating themselves and living life to the full, but they are more likely to seek discounts and schemes to do so. Many different factors feed into these saving tendencies, and most of the time, generational attitudes towards saving can be put down on the state of the economy as a whole during different eras. However, it's all about finding the right balance for you and your personal finances, whatever tribe you are a part of.

## Work Place Impact and Motivators

Each generation's approach to money reflects their unique historical and economic influences, shaping what they consider 'valuable' in their lives. The differing views on money among generations significantly impact workplace dynamics, influencing priorities, decision-making, and workplace culture. Here's how:

Older generations may be more risk-averse and value financial stability and retirement benefits due to their proximity to retirement. They might prioritize salary over perks like wellness programs. While younger generations may be more open to taking risks, like changing jobs for better pay or benefits. Younger generations will also tend to expect transparency around pay and equity and advocate for fair compensation, potentially driving organizational shifts toward open salary discussions. On the other

Older generations may be more risk-averse and value financial stability and retirement benefits due to their proximity to retirement. They might prioritize salary over perks like wellness programs. While younger generations may be more open to taking risks, like changing jobs for better pay or benefits. Younger generations will also tend to expect transparency around pay and equity and advocate for fair compensation, potentially driving organizational shifts toward open salary discussions. On the other hand, older generations might be less inclined toward pay transparency, viewing it as a disruption to traditional hierarchies.

hand, older generations might be less inclined toward pay transparency, viewing it as a disruption to traditional hierarchies. Gen Z and Millennials value investments in social impact and sustainability, expecting companies to allocate funds responsibly. This can clash with older generations who prioritize profitability and traditional financial metrics. This divergence impacts company financial policies, budgeting, and how employees approach innovation or spending. Designing reward systems can become challenging.

To address these generational differences, companies can **Customize Benefits.** They can think of tailored packages addressing diverse financial priorities. HR can also provide resources for all employees to manage personal and professional finances better; facilitate conversations to understand and accommodate differing money mindsets.

## Sustainability

### Boyan Slat and Ocean Clean-up

While on vacation in Greece at 16 years old, Boyan Slat was scuba diving and saw more plastic bags than fish in the sea, which left him thinking, 'Why can't we just clean this up?' He started looking into the problem and possible technological solutions to clean up ocean plastic pollution, dedicating a school project to further developing his idea. He presented his ideas at a TEDx Conference in late 2012. In February 2013, the TEDx video suddenly went viral, and the momentum that followed allowed Boyan to drop out of his Aerospace Engineering degree to officially found The Ocean Cleanup.

Armed with only €300 of saved-up pocket money, Boyan dropped out of his Aerospace Engineering degree at Delft University of Technology and started detailing his plan, but initially struggled to make progress. However, this all changed a few months later when Boyan's TEDx presentation was picked up and publicized by various news blogs, pushing the video around the world and causing the idea to go viral. This momentum allowed Boyan to assemble an initial team of volunteers and launch a crowdfunding campaign that funded a year-long feasibility study – the first real step in bringing Boyan's technological solutions to life. This is how The Ocean Cleanup started. The Ocean Cleanup is actively cleaning up the Great Pacific Garbage Patch and has deployed interceptors in some of the world's most polluting rivers to prevent plastic from reaching the ocean in the first place.

## Gen Z and Climate

I live in the western-most state of India (the state of Gujarat or the land of Gandhi) which has pretty tropical weather most of the year. The state has a coastline to the Arabian Sea, but we are inland in the center of the state. We effectively have three seasons: summer, brief monsoons and spring. Note: I have not mentioned winters as a season because the temperatures rarely go below 10° C, which makes it more like spring. Historically, our summer temperatures are around 37-38C, and monsoons are quite normal (i.e. 6-8 weeks of rain) from July to August. However, over the last several years, all of us have been experiencing extreme weather patterns in India. Summers are becoming excruciatingly hot, with temperatures crossing 47-48° C and monsoons going completely dry or to the other extreme where floods occur. My son, who is otherwise very easygoing about weather, has been complaining about the hot weather nonstop. His walk from college is short, but the stinging heat makes him feel that this climate crisis is something his generation will face for a long time to come. He often laments to me that his generation is paying the price for the crimes done by my generation.

As a Generation Xer, and knowing other Boomers, the climate crisis or the severity of it was never a topic of discussion. Today, it seems everyone is feeling it. From scorching wildfires in Canada and Greece that destroyed vast forests and forced evacuations to record-breaking floods in China and Libya that swept away homes and claimed thousands of lives, climate change is increasingly impacting communities on every continent. The Himalayan regions have seen devastating glacial melts leading to flash floods, while extreme heat waves in parts of the US and Europe have stressed energy grids and intensified drought conditions. Coastal cities are witnessing rising sea levels, threatening millions with displacement and economic disruption.

The climate crisis is quite real, and the Gen Z experiencing this most intensely in their 20s really values those doing something to protect Mother Earth. They fear that if we don't stop or slow down, the Earth may not be livable in the next few years. So, it is 'VALUE' they expect their employers to endorse. So, the next time a Gen Z inquiries about the sustainability drive, we know the background.

The climate crisis is quite real, and the Gen Z experiencing this most intensely in their 20s really values those doing something to protect Mother Earth. They fear that if we don't stop or slow down, the Earth may not be livable in the next few years. So, it is 'VALUE' they expect their employers to endorse.

As for other generations sustainability matters too, but they have a slightly different lens.

**Boomers:** For Baby Boomers, who came of age during pivotal movements like the Civil Rights era and the rise of environmental awareness, sustainability represents a moral responsibility. Many Boomers have witnessed environmental degradation and responded by embracing the early principles of conservation, recycling, and social responsibility. However, their approach tends to be pragmatic and incremental, supporting policies and practices that are proven effective over time.

**Xers:** Generation X grew up in the shadow of economic downturns, corporate scandals, and evolving environmental awareness. They often approach sustainability with a strategic, bottom-line mindset, emphasizing how sustainable practices can enhance efficiency, reduce costs, and promote innovation. For Gen X, sustainability is not only an ethical concern but also a practical approach to safeguarding future resources.

**Gen Y's:** Millennials came of age during a time of increasing social consciousness and digital connectivity, where global issues like Climate Change became part of everyday discourse. For them, sustainability is intrinsically linked to a sense of purpose, justice, and global citizenship. Many Millennials see sustainability as an essential factor in job satisfaction, seeking employers whose values align with their own commitment to the planet and social equity.

**Gen Z** as we've seen earlier, the youngest workforce cohort, has been raised in a digital world where climate urgency is a prominent and pressing issue. Having grown up with school climate strikes, Greta Thunberg's activism, and the effects of climate change, Gen Z views sustainability with a sense of immediacy. They value organizations that take a proactive stance on sustainability and expect swift, innovative solutions to environmental issues. Gen Z employees are often vocal advocates for adopting sustainable technology, investing in renewable energy, and embracing ethical business practices. They view sustainability as a matter of survival rather than preference and are drawn to companies that adopt bold, transformative approaches. For them, traditional business practices must evolve rapidly to meet the demands of a sustainable future. Transparency, authenticity, and commitment to environmental and social justice are key factors in their loyalty to an employer.

## Sustainability and Impact at Work

Generations differ sharply on sustainability's role at work, creating both friction and opportunity. One can see differing levels of activism on sustainability. For example, the Boomers and Xers often see sustainability as a compliance issue rather than a mission-driven cause. It is good as a bonus, not a core focus.

Millennials and Gen Z, however, view sustainability as non-negotiable, expecting companies to champion environmental responsibility and often expecting employers to adopt eco-friendly policies such as reducing carbon footprints, waste, and energy consumption. This generational divide can strain collaboration but also drive action as younger employees push for meaningful, systemic change. They hold organizations accountable for their environmental impact. For one of our clients (a global waste management company), recruiting young employees has generally not been an issue because everyone who is passionate about climate change is keen to join.

Companies that recognize these differences and position sustainability as both a business and an ethical imperative can unify teams and meet evolving expectations. Organizations that have failed to incorporate sustainability into their brand often struggle to attract younger talent, affecting long-term growth.

> Companies that recognize these differences and position sustainability as both a business and an ethical imperative can unify teams and meet evolving expectations. Organizations that have failed to incorporate sustainability into their brand often struggle to attract younger talent, affecting long-term growth.

In working with India's largest waste management firm over the last few years, we have learned some of the best practices adopted by them. One of the key ways to address generational differences in sustainability is to foster dialogue and understand different perspectives. It is important to educate employees on the business case for sustainability and its long-term benefits, create a multi-generational task force to design sustainability programs and highlight both the immediate and future impacts which appeal to everyone. All of this, if done right, can build a shared sense of purpose but also strengthen the overall sustainability journey.

## Relationships

---

### Personal Story

I relocated to India after 15 years in the U.S. due to a tragic car accident in which I lost my mother. My father, who was disabled in the accident, spent the next 20 remaining years in India, and we lived with him in our house in India. He was in his mid-50s when this happened. In 2020, I lost him at the age of 76 owing to many health and age-related issues. At his funeral, I saw over 900+ people come from different phases of his life to pay respect to him – people who knew him from his professional working days, his college days, his students, his clients, friends from childhood, people from our native place and others. It was undoubtedly a testimony of the relationships he had built in his lifetime.

We've seen him many times opening up his old book of contacts (his Rolodex) and calling people routinely to check on them to see how they were doing. One thing that struck my son, nephew, and the rest of the house and me during our time together was how he and his two brothers spoke to each other with undeterred regularity – every single day, 365 days a year. Even if it was a brief conversation, there was a daily chat. Obviously, you can wonder what one would talk about in a daily phone call or if this was possible because they were at the end of their professional careers and had time. Either way, it is a value we want to emulate in the second and third generations. Our relationship with the second and third generations is also close, given we all leverage technology (FaceTime, WhatsApp), but it is the elders in the house who have anchored us. We owe it to them. Their message about the importance of building and keeping relations comes out loud and clear, and it is the connection between good and bad times that strengthens the ties.

So, do all generations see the importance of relationships differently? And what is the corollary of this at the workplace?

Let's examine each generation, their context and their take on relationships.

**Boomers**: For this generation, relationships are often defined by loyalty, trust, and longevity. They value deep, meaningful connections built over time, with a strong emphasis on in-person interactions and shared experiences. They tend to prioritize loyalty in both personal and professional relationships, often fostering close ties with colleagues, clients, and friends over many years. In the workplace, they view relationships as essential to building credibility and respect, believing that trust is earned through consistency and dedication.

**Xers**: Gen X grew up with a balance of traditional in-person relationships and the beginnings of digital communication, such as email and early social media. This generation values independence and tends to approach relationships with a pragmatic mindset, often seeking a balance between personal boundaries and meaningful connections. In the workplace, Gen Xers appreciate strong, supportive professional networks but prefer to build relationships selectively. They value reliability and professionalism in others and are often wary of overly hierarchical or superficial connections.

**Gen Y**: This generation came of age with the rise of digital communication, social media, and a cultural shift toward collaboration. They value relationships that align with their sense of purpose and identity, seeking connections that are authentic, inclusive, and growth-oriented. For Millennials, relationships in the workplace are central to job satisfaction and personal fulfilment. They tend to value transparency, openness, and empathy in both personal and professional interactions and are often driven by a desire to make meaningful contributions to their networks.

**Gen Z**: As the first fully digital generation, Generation Z has grown up with smartphones, social media, and instant communication. For them, relationships are fluid and flexible, with a high value placed on authenticity and directness. Gen Z values genuine connections, often preferring quality over quantity in their relationships despite their extensive online presence. They are comfortable with both digital and face-to-face interactions but prioritize transparency and open communication in all relationships. In the workplace, Gen Z seeks an inclusive environment where they feel respected and valued, expecting honest feedback and open dialogue.

## Impact at Work

In today's world, staying connected with family and friends has become easier than ever before through social media. We have access to their whereabouts, updates, developments and the latest happenings, making it easy to stay updated with their lives. However, just staying connected is not enough to build relationships. To maintain a strong connection, we need to continually work on the relationships we share.

This also applies to the workplace as well. So, whether it is the boss-subordinate, peer-to-peer, or external stakeholders like customers, suppliers, regulators, or others, it is only continuous dialogue and connection that make a strong relationship. Some of the best leaders are those (irrespective of the generation they come from) who have built relations. For firms, bridging these gaps means cultivating a culture of empathy, adaptability, and mutual respect across generations. Companies that foster cross-generational mentorship and respect each group's style can build a culture where all generations feel valued and connected.

Some of the best leaders are those (irrespective of the generation they come from) who have built relations. For firms, bridging these gaps means cultivating a culture of empathy, adaptability, and mutual respect across generations. Companies that foster cross-generational mentorship and respect each group's style can build a culture where all generations feel valued and connected.

Finally, I share with you two simple 2 × 2 frameworks you can use in the evaluation of your relations:

- In the first frame, you can examine your relations with the different stakeholders in the professional context. (Fig.1.0)
- The second one is more general on 'relationships' and can be applied professionally and personally. (Fig.1.1)

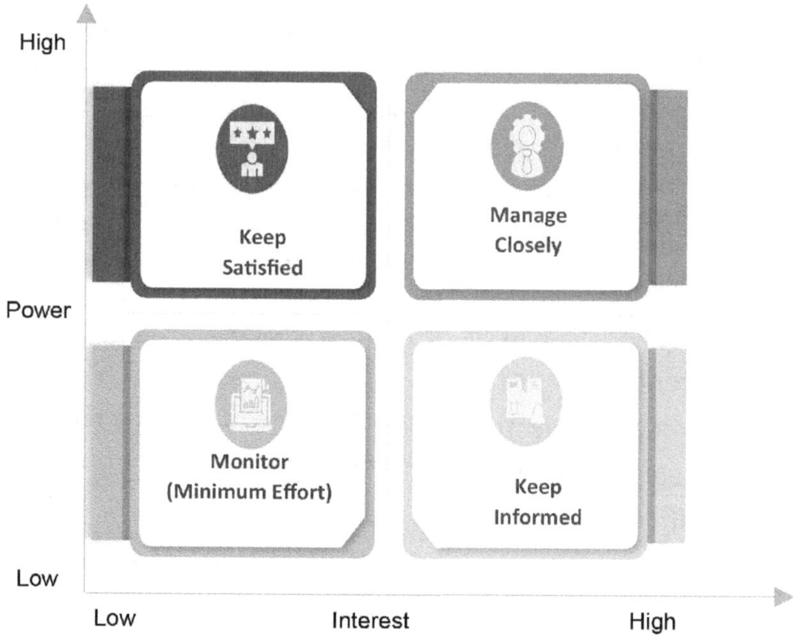


Fig 1.0 Evaluating Relations and Effective Stakeholder Management

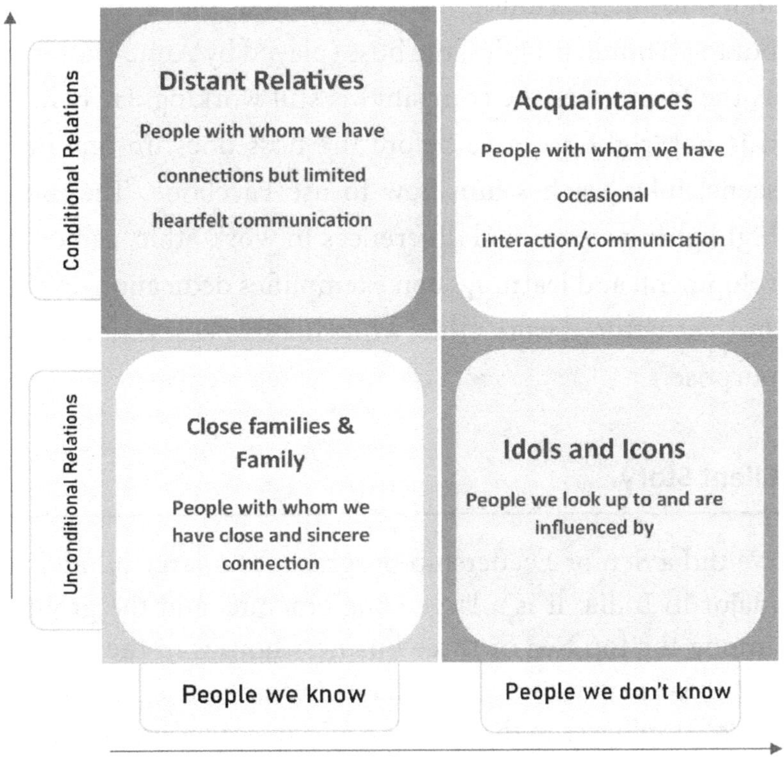


**Fig 1.1 Framework for Relations in Personal Life**

## Work Ethic, Career Development and Learning

In the 2015 movie *The Intern* starring Robert DeNiro (who plays the role of a retired widower as Ben) finds himself bored with retirement. He applies to a newly conceived position of 'senior intern' at a fast-growing e-commerce start-up founded by Millennials in Brooklyn. When being interviewed for the position, he mentions he spent his entire career with one company for more than 20+ years which comes as a huge shock to the recruiting team. In another scene, he decides not to go home till Jules, the boss (played by Anne Hatheway as the founder of the company) is still working. He believes it is not 'right' to leave before the boss does. In one more scene, Jules teaches him how to use Facebook. The movie highlights generational differences in work ethic, career development, and learning. Ben exemplifies dedication, loyalty, and a structured work ethic, while Jules values flexibility and purpose.

## Client Story

We did a Senior Leadership program for a large oil and gas major in India. It is a large conglomerate, and the group is among the top two or three business houses in the country. The O&G firm is one of their flagship companies. The average age of employees in that firm is 68. Many of the executives are from the time of the founder, and almost 98% of the people we spoke to have spent their entire working career with the firm. The founder had the philosophy that if people are good and willing to work hard, they should be kept, groomed, and allowed to work as long as they desire. The firm also often paid 2x or 3x what the competition would have paid in many roles. In view of this the employees showed full dedication to the firm and the owner. They were often seen working very late, on weekends and as needed or called upon (which was the implicit culture) to get things 'done.' Many executives said this with pride and often quoted that it is their hard work that has helped them grow through the ranks. As the firm was developing this senior group, they had also identified a group of executives who were in their mid-40s and being groomed for senior leadership. These were mid-career executives who had worked in other oil and gas companies (private or public) and had joined this firm. While they were also willing to work hard, they had a different vision of their career, how much to work hard versus smart work and how to leverage the technology in their area of work. For the older population a new role was how they saw investment in themselves and 'learning' would happen, and most of the time, it was 'on the job.' For the Millennials, there was an expectation of formal classroom training, attending a workshop at a top B school or Ivy League Advanced Management Program and learning from experts who brought management stories into the classroom.

This contrast displayed the workplace 'attitude and value' of the two generations. The older generation was the Boomer population and believed that you begin your career with one company and stay with them till retirement. Loyalty was a big factor. Second, the firm would take care of their growth and there was deep respect for the hierarchy. For this particular company investing in the next generation bench which comprised Gen X and Millennials was equally important but they also had to understand the different aspirations and, therefore, adapt accordingly.

Let's look at some of the generational preferences and how they see work ethic, development and learning.

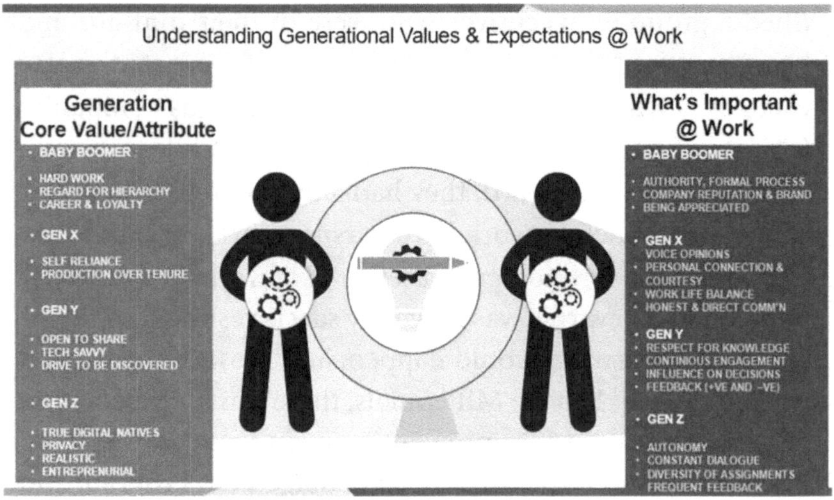


Fig 1.2: Workplace Values of Different Generations

## Boomers: The Climbers

As the story above shows, Boomers equate work with personal identity. They are known for their long hours, drive, and thrive in competitive environments. They believe in paying dues to earn success. For them, career growth is a result of hard work and visible dedication. They seek titles, promotions, and prestige as milestones of accomplishment. To achieve this, they prefer structured training programs but are adaptable to blended methods. They appreciate classroom learning but are open to technology-enhanced options.

## Gen X: The Sandwich Generation and Independent Pragmatists

A couple of years ago, one of the IT scions in India made a comment that youngsters today really need to work long hours to succeed. Putting 70 hours or so in the early part of the career builds a good work ethic and character which will help them grow and succeed in their career. More recently, the chairman of a large construction company indicated that if he could have his way, all employees should come to work every Sunday. 'How long can you look at your spouse on a weekend,' he lamented. Shortly after this comment, social media was abuzz with views and counter-views on what the right number of work hours should be in today's high-paced, high-stress work environment. Is it fair to expect everyone to put in those hours because someone else did? Does climbing the corporate ladder quickly define the success of an individual? Others advocated this school of thought, indicating that in the early days of one's career there is a need to gain experience and work 'more' if needed. Unless you go through the grind success doesn't come. To think success will just come by doing a 9 to 5 kind of routine will not happen.

This comment really stirred the hornet's nest. This was another instance of how different generations saw how much work was enough, good, and required. Is more always better? The Boomer generation saw more hours as a way to demonstrate loyalty, hard work and the growth path. For Generation X – often called the lost generation – it has been a mixed bag when it comes to things like the number of hours, and how they see career development and learning. Often pegged as the 'sandwich' generation they have aging parents on one end and young children to manage on the other. This was the first generation for whom work was truly becoming global. Long hours, different time zones and the need to balance 'work-life' was a term perhaps most suited and created during this generation.

So, having Boomers as bosses, Gen Xers do see the value of hard work, but they are also the generation which views things from a different context. Managing global teams, the flexibility of work hours, using technology and learning online are important to them. They value efficiency, balance, and pragmatism in their approach to work. Working in global firms with international exposure is a way for career development and growth. They prefer lateral moves or entrepreneurial ventures over waiting for promotions. Growth is personal and professional rather than strictly hierarchical.

## Gen Y and Z Career Values: Understanding their Context in the Changing Technological Landscape (AI, ML and others)

A few years ago, the Global Strategy Consulting firm BCG published a report in which they studied roughly 2500 public companies and how they have fared over a 30-year period. The objective was to see which companies have excelled in what they define as 'stable' periods versus turbulent periods. An index was created in which they tracked companies that outperformed their peers relative to their industry during the quarters of highest turbulence in demand, competition and capital market expectations. While the phenomenon of turbulence itself was not new to businesses, its nature and degree had changed significantly over time. In their report they furnished some unsettling facts:

- Turbulence struck more frequently than in the past. More than half of the most turbulent quarters over the past 30 years had occurred during the past decade.
- Turbulence had increased in intensity. Volatility in revenue growth, revenue ranking, and operating margins had more than doubled compared to the 1960s.
- Turbulence today persisted much longer than in preceding periods. The average duration of periods of high turbulence quadrupled over the past three decades.

Among their findings, the companies that adjusted and learned better, faster and more economically than their rivals continued to grow despite the turbulence. Adaptiveness was the new source of competitive advantage.

Noted futurist Heather McGowan beautifully explains how the frequency of change is impacting our need to prepare for the future. This change, therefore, impacts the way organizations think and function. In figure 1.3 we see the two graphs that depict the rate of change against time. The rate of change is moving from a linear to an exponential curve. Singularity University describes linear change as a condition wherein if we moved 30 steps, we would reach 30 meters at the end of the line. Whereas, in the case of exponential change, the covered distance gets doubled at each step. So, if we move 30 exponential steps, we would actually cover a billion meters, which is 26 times around the globe. This is evident in the shrinking time taken for each new invention of technology and its penetration. The telephone took 50 years for 30% penetration. The internet/PC took 20 years, and the mobile took even less time (10 years). This shows that, as humans, we adapt but we adapt at a linear pace; however, technology is changing at an exponential rate.

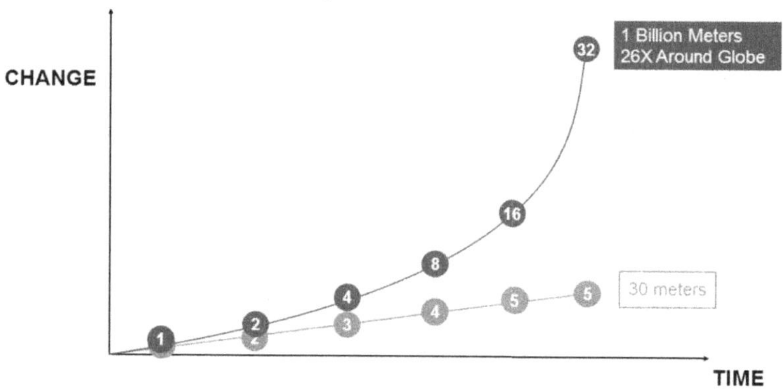

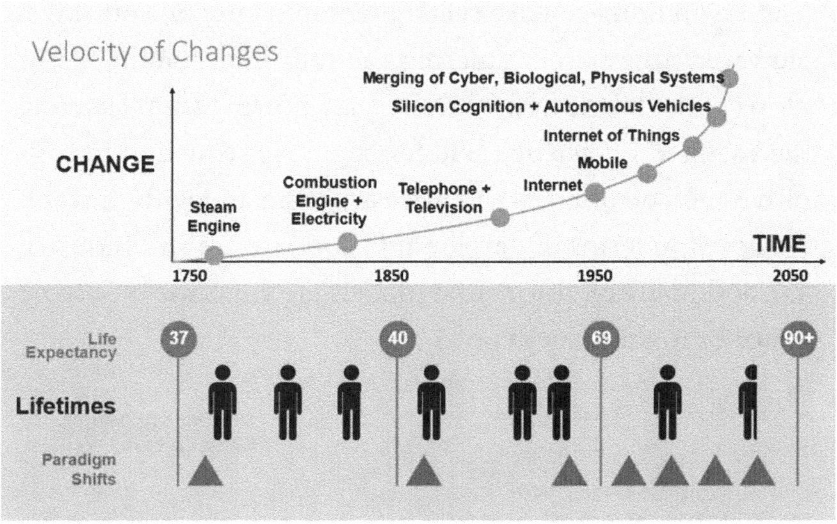


Fig 1.3 Understanding the Speed of Change – Not a Linear Curve (©Heather McGowan)

If we extend the discussion on the canvas of pace and amount of effect, to what extent can change impact the current and future talent? Well, each prior industrial revolution, especially the fourth industrial revolution, has taught us how to employ talent and tools. So, we have gone from steam engines to mass production, then computer automation, and now, we have cyber-physical things such as the Internet of Things. Across each industrial era, the focus of talent has been different. (See Figure 1.4 below).

The current workplace has prepared itself for the last industrial revolution by plunging itself into a deep domain of expertise using Science, Technology, Engineering, and Mathematics (STEM) skills. Therefore, in the fourth industrial revolution, we have relied predominantly on soft skills. However, now we are entering the fifth information age in terms of the talent shift, where we are moving from learning the acquired knowledge skill for cognitive reduction to cognitive augmentation, where we learn from and with the tool. However, in terms of developing talent, we are still Industry 4.0, and many of our mental models are from the industrial era prior to the current one.

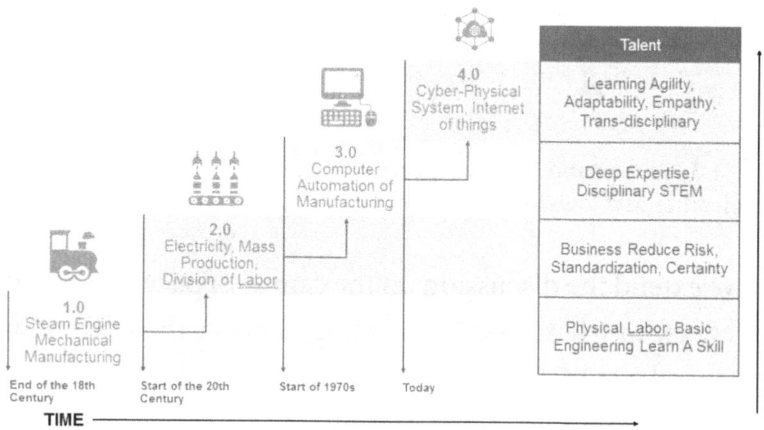


Fig1.4 Talent Expectations in Industry 4.0 ©Heather McGown

## How Will the Gen Y and Z Careers Be Impacted?

Heather McGowan, whom we quoted earlier, states that in the old economy we were educated in one band, we had careers in another band, and then we retired in another band. This means we spent the initial part of our life studying, and that is all we had to worry about. Then we began the career band in which we climbed the career ladder, and finally, we had the third band in which we retired. Success is how we give the knowledge and skills to the individual so it can be translated into the workforce.

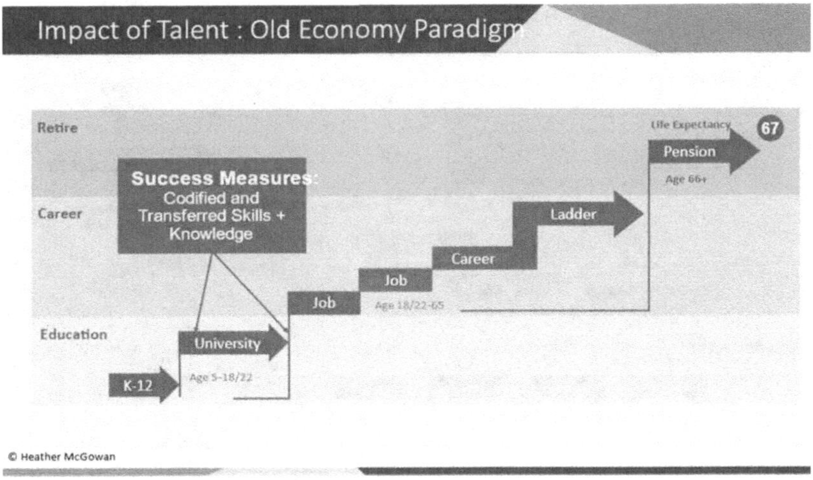


Fig 1.5 Role of Education in Careers ©Heather McGown

**Now, the new paradigm shifts to where we learn.** Success now can be measured by the ability to learn and be agile. This means that the older model of learn-learn-learn needs to be reframed to learn, unlearn and relearn. She also indicates the need to retire the questions to the young students, such as asking them what they want to be when they grow up. According to some statistics, close to 65% of jobs for which they are studying will not be there or be automated. Close to only 27% of people work in their chosen paths of major, and with

Success now can be measured by the ability to learn and be agile. This means that the older model of learn-learn-learn needs to be reframed to learn, unlearn and relearn.

the current change, they are likely to change about 17 jobs across five industries. So, it would be hard to define when someone asked them what it is that they do.

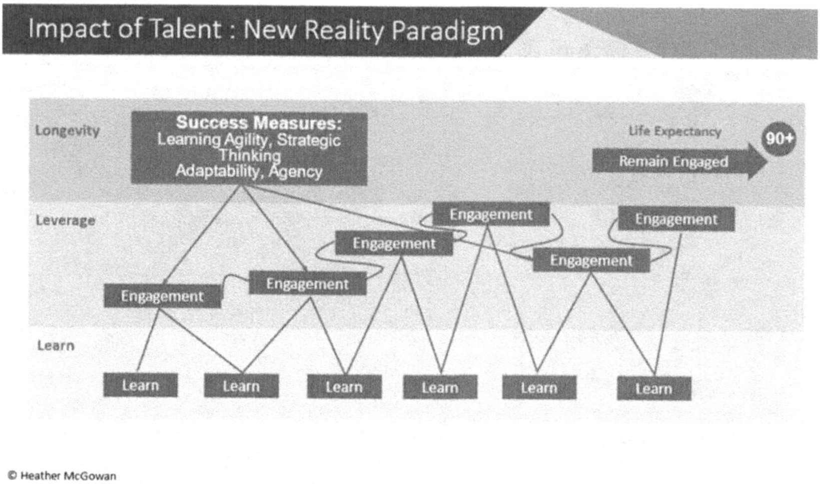


Fig 1.6 Learning Is the New Lever for Careers in a Multi-Gen Workforce ©Heather McGown

## Understanding Gen Y and Z's Work Ethic and Career Development: The Purpose-Driven Collaborators and Agile Innovators

Given this context, what influences Gen Y's and Z's expectations of a career path? The rapid change (especially the learnings from the COVID-19 pandemic) has taught us that problems have to be looked at from multiple dimensions. For example, it wasn't just enough for us to create a good vaccine when the pandemic began. We had to think about ways to shorten the time to create a vaccine. After that, who gets it first? Doctors, senior citizens or adults versus kids? How do we price it? How do we ship it? What will be the communication strategy around it?

This means that one can no longer be an expert in one domain area and expect to solve today's complex problems. Careers, therefore, have to be created in a transdisciplinary way. Employees will have to become more 'agile' in learning and unlearning their past.

This means that one can no longer be an expert in one domain area and expect to solve today's complex problems. Careers, therefore, have to be created in a transdisciplinary way. Employees will have to become more 'agile' in learning and unlearning their past.

Therefore, Gen Y and Z – the two generations most impacted by the changes will not want a traditional grow-in-one-function for 30 years approach. 'Career Lattice' and deliberate cross-functional exposure are becoming the need of the hour. Secondly, COVID-19 has forced many, especially these two generations, to rethink the 'place' of work in their life. How much time do we spend on 'work'? Is it about a bigger pay check, or is it about meaningful work?

So, they value flexibility and meaning in their work. Promotions are less important than growth and impact. Career paths, therefore, are seen as fluid. They seek purpose-driven roles with opportunities for learning and mentorship. Lateral moves and gig opportunities are common preferences.

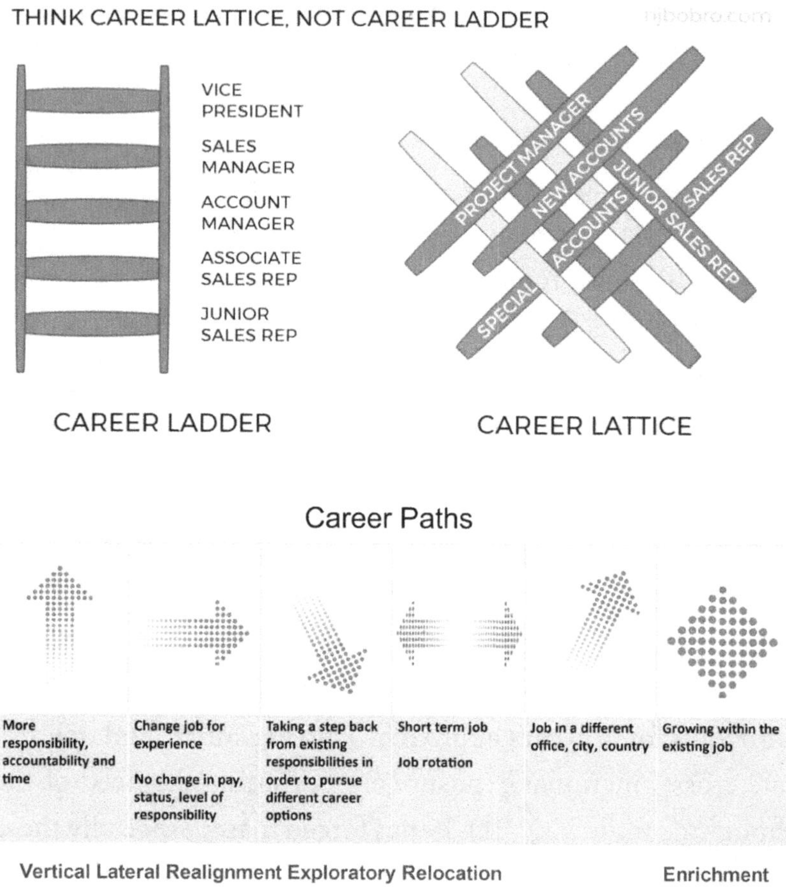


Fig 1.7 Traditional Career vs. Career Lattice. Understanding the Various Career Paths

So, when it comes to work ethic, career growth, and learning, each generation brings a unique perspective. By understanding these differences and adapting strategies to align with them, organizations can bridge generational divides and create an environment where everyone thrives.

Throughout this chapter, we've explored how dimensions like money, sustainability, work ethic, career, and relationships reflect the core values of each generation. However, every generation sees it differently based on their context and story. Yet, these are just a starting point; other areas like communication styles, work preferences, and many others offer even more to uncover. We will examine more dimensions of the workplace with a generation lens, but if all values are seen with curiosity and respect, organizations can harness the richness of generational diversity to create workplaces that are agile, inclusive, and deeply human.

**Examples of how companies are leveraging generational strength for work, career, and learning:**

---

**Work Ethic**

**Boomers:** Value long hours and dedication; equate effort with results.

*Example:* **IBM** encourages recognition of long service and mentorship programs where Boomers share their knowledge with younger employees, respecting their hard-working ethic.

**Gen Xers:** Prefer autonomy and efficiency; prioritize work-life balance.

*Example:* **Microsoft** implements flexible working hours and encourages remote work, appealing to Gen X's preference for autonomy.

**Millennials:** Seek purpose in work; focus on productivity rather than hours worked.

*Example:* **Airbnb** ties company goals to employees' sense of purpose, integrating sustainability initiatives that resonate with Millennials.

**Gen Z:** Emphasize ethical impact, quick results, and adaptability.

*Example:* **Patagonia** focuses on its mission-driven culture, allowing Gen Z to align work with their values.

**Career Development**

**Boomers:** Prefer structured career paths and promotions tied to tenure.

*Example:* **GE** retains Boomers through leadership roles on strategic projects that leverage their experience.

**Gen Xers:** Value opportunities for skill-building and lateral growth.

*Example:* **Deloitte** offers Gen X robust internal mobility programs, enabling them to pivot within the organization.

**Millennials:** Demand frequent feedback, mentorship, and rapid progression.

*Example:* **Google** integrates continuous feedback mechanisms like real-time performance tools and personalized development plans for Millennials.

**Gen Z:** Expect opportunities early and look for roles offering learning and personal branding potential.

*Example:* **TikTok** engages Gen Z by providing platforms for idea ownership and visibility, even for entry-level employees.

**Learning**

**Boomers:** Favor traditional classroom-style or formalized training.

*Example:* **Boeing** offers in-person seminars and certification programs to accommodate Boomers' preferences for structured learning.

**Gen Xers:** Appreciate self-directed e-learning and time-efficient formats.

*Example:* **AT&T** promotes digital self-paced learning modules that fit into Gen X's busy schedules.

**Millennials:** Prefer collaborative and tech-driven learning methods.

*Example:* **LinkedIn Learning** uses AI to suggest content based on Millennial users' professional goals.

**Gen Z:** Thrive on micro-learning and gamification via digital platforms.

*Example:* **PwC** incorporates gamified learning platforms to teach skills, such as data analytics, tailored for Gen Z's short attention spans.

## What Companies Have Done to Bridge These Differences

1. **SAP:** Launched multi-generational collaboration initiatives, encouraging cross-generational teams to co-develop solutions and share knowledge.
2. **Cisco:** Created reverse mentorship programs where younger employees teach Boomers and Gen X about emerging technologies, and vice versa for leadership skills.
3. **Unilever:** Established 'Future Fit' learning programs catering to all generations, combining structured programs for Boomers and self-paced, app-based modules for younger employees.
4. **EY:** Offers initiatives like 'Belonging through Generations,' fostering dialogues on generational perspectives and aligning career expectations.

CHAPTER 2

# The Hybrid Realities: How Generations Collide and Lessons from the Office-Hybrid Evolution

'Workplaces will need to shift from measuring input to measuring output—trusting employees to manage their time in ways that achieve results.'

*Ginni Rometty (former CEO of IBM)*

## Client Story

It was January 2022 and I was invited to speak for a virtual session by SLASSCOM. This is Sri Lanka's largest IT body which represents its IT firms as a cluster for outsourcing work and framing IT company policies. The topic I was going to cover was **'Leadership Challenges in a Hybrid Working World.'** There was a huge curiosity as we had close to 5000 attendees across Asia on this webinar. By then, much of the world had seen at least two waves of COVID-19 and possibly three for many. People were not sure if the end was in sight, and companies had a realization that getting people back to offices (full-time) was not going to happen anytime soon like in the pre-COVID days. But at the same time, many had never experienced such an extended period of time where the entire workforce had to work remotely. Many companies were hopeful that as COVID-19 slowly showed signs of abating that things would return to normal. But what would 'normal' look like if people kept the past 18 months as a reference point? By then, most companies were working hard to find ways to serve customers remotely, conduct team meetings, collaborate through technology and even conduct employee appraisals online. This experience was quite mixed, and several doubts lingered on the best way to adapt to this new way of working and what the future might look like.

Later that year, we resumed doing face-to-face workshops for clients, and we were conducting a year-long program for a wind energy firm. It was for their senior managers and had many topics for a year-long intervention. One of the things they were struggling with was to attract young talent to have a career in manufacturing. So, we had invited about a dozen people in the room who were freshly recruited to conduct a talk-show-like discussion on what their career aspirations would look like. In addition to all the things that came out on the expectations from an employer – engagement in the role, diversity of assignments, timely feedback, an opportunity to learn, etc. – one thing that emerged quite prominently was the flexibility to work from home, for example, come in late during non-traffic hours and work till late. The company didn't have a clear-cut policy yet and kept the pre-COVID norms. Employees were expected to come in by 9 am and leave by 6 pm. However, this wasn't going down well for many fresh recruits; in two years, half of the freshly recruited management trainees had quit. Lack of flexibility with working hours was the primary reason for this exit.

In another story, one of the largest IT firms in India took a call at the onset of COVID-19 to say that they would stop investing in new offices. This meant there would be no new physical offices by 2025. This company has offices in more than 25 countries and has publicly coined the slogan '25 by 25', which means that only 25 % of the workforce will have to be in offices by 2025, and working remotely will be the way of the future. However, things didn't quite go as they had planned. In fact, it went for a complete 180-degree change just within a year. The firm noticed that by giving everyone the flexibility of working from home, young IT engineers were making themselves available for 'freelancing' projects to other firms and using any idle time in the evening or day to procure more work. Their own work also suffered due to the remote way of working. At first, it seemed like an anomaly, but it was distinctly becoming a pattern in the industry. In early 2024, the company made 'back to office' mandatory, and employees had to adhere to a five-day week. A part of their variable pay was also linked to office attendance.

This was the spectrum of how the post-COVID-19 work would look: from offering some flexibility of working from home to full flexibility of being fully remote to bringing everyone back to the office 100%.

## Evaluating Hybrid Models: Benefits and Trade-Offs

As the world came out of the COVID-19 pandemic, the shift to hybrid work became one of the most significant changes in workplace dynamics. Three or four distinct models of working emerged. Some of these models offer greater flexibility but also pose new challenges, particularly in managing a workforce composed of multiple generations with differing expectations, values, and work habits.

Let's first list out the various models being practiced by organizations:

1. **At-Will Model** (also often called Flexible Hybrid): Employees decide where they work.
2. **The Split Week Model:** (also called Fixed Hybrid) Set days in office, set days remote.
3. **Fully Remote:** Employees work remotely by default and go to the office occasionally.
4. **Fully At-Office:** Employees have to work in the office as the primary way of working, and remote is an option (only on some days or in certain situations).
5. **Shift-Work:** Employees choose a certain shift (mornings or evenings) and get work done if their role allows them this flexibility.
6. **Week-by-Week:** Employees come to the office for a week and work remotely for a week (similar to Fixed Hybrid) contingent upon the role.

## Personal Story

In the early 2000s, I recall working in the Internal Audit Department of Charles Schwab, a large brokerage firm in San Francisco. We were a motley crew of 150 people (sort of like a company within a company on the island) because people did not see auditors as very friendly people. There, we tried a practice which was perhaps much ahead of its time. We implemented what was called the '9/80 rule'. The 9/80 rule essentially involved finishing 80 hours in nine days and getting the tenth day off. This went away from the traditional 40 hours in one week or 80 hours in 2 weeks (10 days). As a result, every alternate Friday was a holiday, and we would get a long weekend. This meant that each day was longer than the traditional eight hours, closer to nine hours. These days, nine hours can be seen as normal at many companies, given client deliverables and the need to collaborate across time zones. At first, there were questions: Would this hamper client deadlines and the work? Would people misuse this privilege by taking personal holidays always with the long weekend, and be gone for three-four days at a stretch? But the data was to the contrary.

After about six months into the practice, the Audit Head shared in our internal town hall that productivity was at an all-time high as this was a pilot and an experiment. The productivity here was measured by the number of audits we had to complete and reports generated to the committee in a given quarter for each team. This would include meeting stakeholders, identifying issues, recommending solutions and ensuring that the implementation was done on time.

By the end of the year, our group seemed to be the happiest in the firm. Everyone who knew an auditor from our team always saw them smiling (not the image people carried about us). This led to a stark realization – flexibility came with great responsibility. This was a perk, and it would be taken away if people did not show maturity towards their work and deliverables. Trust was given to us by our management and accountability had to be given back to them in return. Eventually, this practice gained the attention of other departments and was also being tried. Incidentally, in those three years, the firm was rated among the best employers for three consecutive years.

This led to a stark realization – flexibility came with great responsibility. This was a perk, and it would be taken away if people did not show maturity towards their work and deliverables. Trust was given to us by our management and accountability had to be given back to them in return.

## Hybrid Work – Pains and Gains. What Works and Doesn't

As we fast-forward ourselves to the experience of COVID-19 and post-pandemic, a whole big debate of what the 'workplace' will look like in the corporate world is on the right formula. Let's first see the general benefits and drawbacks of hybrids, and then we will examine if there is a Generational Lens to the workplace and how companies are going about solving this puzzle.

## First the Advantages

**Flexibility for Work-Life Balance:** Employees can adjust their schedules to meet personal and professional demands, reducing burnout. Hybrid empowers workers to tailor their workdays around peak productivity times, whether at home or in the office.

**Increased Productivity:** For many, working remotely eliminates distractions and offers better focus. Employees save commuting time, which they can redirect towards deep work or personal well-being, improving overall performance.

**Cost Savings for Employers and Employees:** Companies can save on office overheads like rent, utilities, and supplies. Similarly, employees save on commuting expenses, meals, and work attire, contributing to financial well-being.

**Wider Talent Pool:** Organizations are no longer limited by geography and can attract talent from different regions. This access to a global workforce can also increase diversity and innovation within teams.

**Reduced Environmental Impact:** Fewer commutes mean lower carbon emissions, aligning companies with sustainability goals. The hybrid model contributes to greener business practices and resonates with environmentally conscious employees.

**Now let's look at the Cons.**_

---

**Communication and Coordination Issues:** Teams can struggle with misalignment when some members are in the office and others remote, leading to slower decision-making. Important information might be lost or delayed in hybrid meetings.

**Weaker Collaboration and Innovation:** Creative problem-solving often benefits from spontaneous interactions and brainstorming, which may be harder to replicate in a hybrid setup. Team cohesion can suffer when employees lack regular face-to-face contact.

**Employee Disconnection and Isolation:** Remote workers, especially new hires or younger employees, might feel disconnected from company culture or excluded from informal networks. This can affect motivation and engagement over time.

**Unequal Workload or Recognition Issues:** Employees working in the office may feel they are contributing more, while remote workers might fear they're missing out on career growth opportunities. The perception of favoritism can affect morale.

**Complex Management and Performance Tracking:** Leaders may find it difficult to track performance, provide timely feedback, and maintain engagement across dispersed teams. Hybrid management requires new skills, tools, and trust to be effective.

## The Generational Lens to Hybrid

Microsoft CEO Satya Nadella gave a very riveting talk somewhere in the middle of the Pandemic on what will be the most important competency for managers of the future. A few months into the Pandemic finding the right formula was difficult for many companies, including Microsoft. Should it be all remote and from home, or should it be all from the office? If it was hybrid, how would employees who had to come to work feel versus those who could work from home? How do you go about collaborating and working in these conditions? It looked like this was the preview of things to come. But all of this was very context-driven due to the differing expectations of employees at different levels and the different generations. (See Fig.2 below)

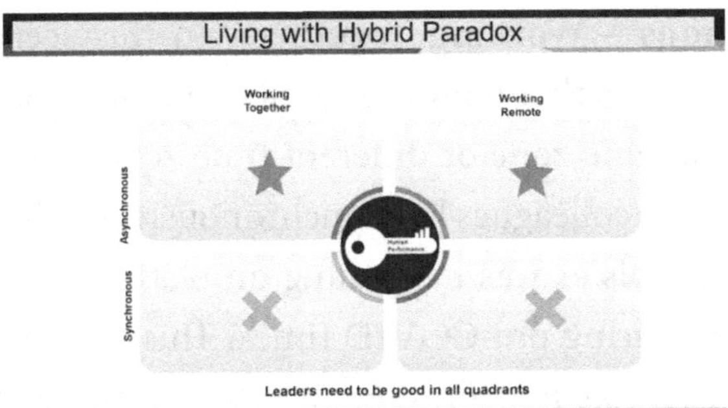


Fig 2.0 Leading in the Hybrid World

Here the four options say:

Asynchronous: Not happening at the same time
Synchronous: Occurring at the same time

**Asynchronous – Working Together**: So, if you are working for a multinational or a global company and have a team in multiple time zones, you are coming to the office, but it may not be possible for everyone to attend your meetings due to the late night/early morning time zones of being in different markets. In this case, oftentimes, the call is recorded on a collaboration platform (like Teams/Zoom), and the colleagues can catch the minutes of a meeting through a recording later on from a shared server.

We saw this regularly for a global bank as many leaders were based in Asia but had teams in more than four or five countries where a live meeting wasn't always possible to attend as it could be an early morning meeting in Asia which was often late evening or night for colleagues in the West (US or Europe).

**Synchronous – Working Together:** In this scenario, you are working together (coming to the office and you could be in the same time zone or different time zones), and you are connecting to colleagues live synchronously but through collaboration tools as was happening on platforms like Webex and others during pre-COVID times. This is when you had teams in multiple locations, but everyone couldn't be physically present in one location.

**Asynchronous – Remote**: Here, similar to the first scenario, you could be in multiple time zones but now working remotely and not coming to the office, so you catch up on the office or client meetings via recordings again.

**Synchronous – Remote**: Finally, this is the most common way of connecting today in hybrid practices which is where some part of the team or entire team are remote but speaking to bosses, subordinates, and customers through collaboration tools.

What Nadella was highlighting is the leadership challenge of leading a team in post-COVID times. So, gone were the days where a manager could take the view, 'I will only join if the team is in the office or will do so if only working remotely.' One had to become good at all four quadrants, which means leading physical teams synchronously and asynchronously, and also remote teams synchronously and asynchronously. And this was not just in dealing with their own team mem-

What Nadella was highlighting is the leadership challenge of leading a team in post-COVID times. So, gone were the days where a manager could take the view, 'I will only join if the team is in the office or will do so if only working remotely.' One had to become good at all four quadrants, which means leading physical teams synchronously and asynchronously, and also remote teams synchronously and asynchronously. And this was not just in dealing with their own team members, but also dealing with peers, bosses, customers and, most importantly, managing themselves in these conditions.

bers, but also dealing with peers, bosses, customers and, most importantly, managing themselves in these conditions.

We now dive deeper into how this was primarily shaped by the differing preferences of generations at the workplace. Here's an overview of how these generational contexts shape their hybrid work preferences, along with examples of how companies adapt their strategies accordingly. We will dive deeper into understanding generational context again in a later chapter.

### Baby Boomers (1946-1964)

**Context**: Baby Boomers grew up in a world where in-person work was the standard, and there was a strong emphasis on loyalty and face-to-face collaboration. For many Boomers, the physical office is synonymous with professionalism and productivity, and they often value structured schedules.

**Hybrid Preference**: Generally, Boomers prefer a structured hybrid model that includes regular office attendance. This approach allows them to maintain social connections and feel more in control, especially given concerns about remote work leading to a sense of isolation or sidelining in promotions.

**Example**: IBM has implemented a hybrid approach for many of its employees but has also encouraged senior leadership and certain teams to work on-site more frequently to foster in-person mentorship and collaboration, appealing to Boomers who value face-to-face interactions.

### Generation X (1965-1980)

**Context**: Gen Xers are known for being self-reliant and adaptable, traits cultivated during a time when both parents often worked, leading them to develop independence early on. They value work-life balance and autonomy in the workplace.

**Hybrid Preference**: Gen X often prefers a flexible hybrid model that allows them to manage both family and work responsibilities without a rigid schedule. This generation is also often known as the 'Sandwich Generation' as they either have young children or elderly parents they are managing. Due to these responsibilities, they appreciate the choice of where and when to work, as long as it doesn't come at the expense of productivity.

**Example**: PepsiCo has designed a 'Work that Works' policy, allowing employees to coordinate directly with managers on in-office and remote schedules. This approach resonates with Gen Xers who prioritize results over hours logged, and it has been popular with this cohort as it fosters independence and balance.

## Millennials (1981-1996)

**Context**: Millennials are digital natives who value flexibility, purpose, and career growth opportunities. They view work as an integral part of life, and many value the freedom to structure their work around personal priorities.

**Hybrid Preference**: Millennials tend to prefer hybrid models with maximum flexibility, often enjoying the ability to work remotely more frequently. However, they also value in-person collaboration for team-building and networking, which they view as vital to career advancement.

**Example**: Salesforce introduced a 'Success from Anywhere' model, empowering employees to choose how they work best while still organizing regular team gatherings for social cohesion and innovation. This model appeals to Millennials, who prefer the flexibility to work from anywhere but also value periodic in-person interactions.

## Generation Z (1997-2012)

**Context**: Gen Z entered the workforce during a time of rapid digital transformation, and many started their careers remotely due to the pandemic. They highly value technology integration and seek employers offering flexible, inclusive, and purpose-driven work environments.

**Hybrid Preference**: Gen Z generally favor remote work for its convenience and flexibility, but they often seek more in-person interactions than Millennials to build a sense of community and belonging. They're open to working from the office if it fosters social connections, learning, and mentorship opportunities.

**Example**: Google has maintained its campus-based culture while offering flexible hybrid work options, allowing employees to come in based on their team's needs. For Gen Z employees, Google offers spaces for collaboration and innovation, which provides them with a balance between digital autonomy and physical community.

Here is how some of the companies redefined how they see the 'office' place. (All remote, all office or hybrid practices).

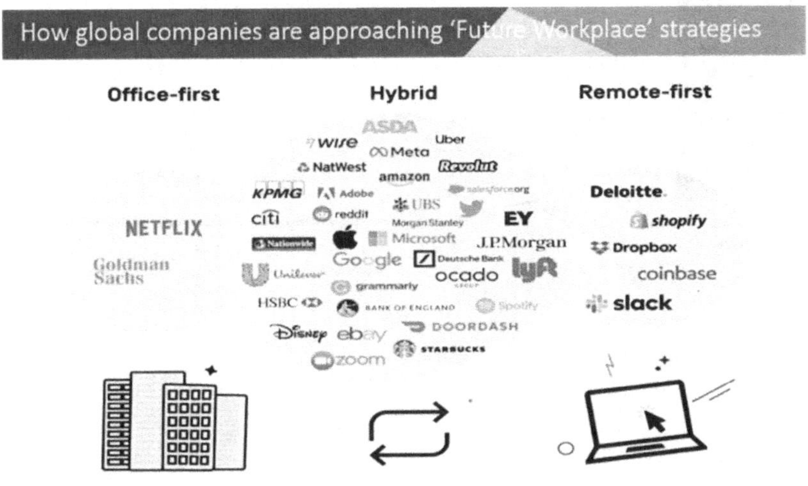


Fig 2.1 Companies with their Decision to Go Remote, Hybrid or Back to Office

| | | Back to Office Approach | Leadership Take |
|---|---|---|---|
| Office First | Goldman Sachs | • Expecting all employees to be back at office | I would certainly expect a lot of Goldman Sachs to be back in fully by end of year. In person is integral to the "Eco-System" of the world. – David Solomon (CEO) |
| | Netflix | • Cast and Crew needed to be fully vaccinated (during Covid-19) in order to work in Studios | Don't see any positives in working from home. Not being able to work in person particularly internationally is negative – Reed Hastings |
| Remote First | Slack | • All Employees have the option to work from Home | There will be face-2-face meetings but primarily for team building and project Kick-offs – Stewart Butterfield (Former CEO) |
| | Shopify | • Allowing all 5000 Employees to work from home indefinitely and reduce office capacity by 20-25% | We will adopt "Digital by Default" mindset and adjust to remote environment – CEO Tobi Lutke |

## Hybrid Practices : Examples

| Company | Hybrid Approach | Leadership Take |
|---|---|---|
| Ericsson | • Cutting Desk Space by 40% globally<br>• 50% of 102 K Workforce to be Remote<br>• Redesigning 400 of the Offices globally | "You will have a chair when you come to office, but instead of going to your old desk, you may be sitting in a conference room or a lounge area " Peter Martin – Head of Managed Services |
| Citi Group | • Data Center and Branch Employees to Go Back to Office<br>• US: 2 Days / week<br>• UK : Work 3 days / week from office | Each Role in Bank renamed to " Hybrid", "Remote" or "Resident" |
| HSBC | • Hong Kong : 30% of employees to work from Offices<br>• Other Locations – Employees choose with approval of Manger | Global CEO Noel Quin indicated he and his leadership team will have a "fully open office – with no designated desks upon returning". Everyone will "Hot Desk" to promote Hybrid and collaboration |

**Hybrid Practices : Examples**

| Company | Hybrid Approach | Leadership Take |
|---|---|---|
| Google | • 3 Days in Office / 2 Days from wherever most comfortable<br>• 60% in office, 20% from New Locations, 20% from Home<br>• 4 Weeks per Year – work from anywhere (with or without pandemic) | • Google uses Camp Fire method<br>• Allows for better Face-2-face<br>• Interactions and distancing |
| TCS / Infosys | • The 25 * 25 Policy : No more than 25% of company's associate to work from anytime and they need not spend more than 25% of time in office | TCS: 3 E's : Enable, Embrace, Empower<br>Infosys : Employees in Development Centers come 2 days/ week.<br>Others come based on role and approval of manager |
| Unilever | • Experimenting in some markets 4 days / week (9/80) Work 9 days and 80 hours<br>• Each country takes their own approach based on the local covid situation | We never expect going back to 5 days a week. But Unilever is keen to return in some offices after seeing a 'slow erosion of capital' – Alan Jope (CEO) |

Fig 2.2 Workplace Decisions at the Onset of COVID-19

Companies committed this as their approach to the workplace at the onset of COVID-19. However, firms quickly started realizing the 'generational' lens to work preferences made it hard to create a one-size-fits-all type of solution. Boomers, who had traditionally preferred 'in-office,' were slowly getting comfortable working from home. Gen Z who were always comfortable working remotely started feeling the pangs of isolation and could not experience the 'company culture.' How do we recruit new talent? Should it be all remote/office or hybrid? How would innovation happen in an organization when everything was done remotely? Numerous surveys and studies started showing that all generations felt ideas were best generated in person. Collaboration would be easier if in the office. So, companies had to revisit and refine their approach to how the office would look like in the future.

## Who's In, When and How – Building Inclusive Hybrid Models for Each Generation

Given the varying needs, firms had to design hybrid models that offered both structure and flexibility, allowing each cohort to thrive. A successful hybrid model, therefore, wasn't just about location, it was about bridging the preferences and needs of every generation. The success of hybrid work depends on creating thoughtful practices that align with both organizational goals and employee well-being. Implementing a sustainable model required considering who should be in the office and when, and most importantly, how work can be managed to maximize productivity while meeting individual and team needs. Let's explore these dimensions in detail.

### Who Should Be in the Office?

A key aspect of hybrid models is determining which roles or individuals benefit most from in-person work. Some positions require greater physical presence, such as roles in operations, client-facing functions, or those that depend on access to specific tools or equipment. Meanwhile, knowledge workers may find working remotely just as efficient, if not more.

- **Boomers and Gen X employees** may prefer in-office work due to the comfort of traditional environments and the chance for face-to-face collaboration.

- **Millennials and Gen Z** lean toward remote or flexible schedules, valuing autonomy and digital tools. However, younger employees may need in-person days for mentorship, learning opportunities, and networking that are harder to replicate remotely.

Creating a role-based or task-based framework helps ensure that in-office presence adds real value, whether for specific projects, collaborative meetings, or learning events.

## When Should Work Happen In-Office Versus Remotely?

Healthy hybrid practices rely on establishing clear guidelines about when employees should be in the office and when remote work is appropriate. The 'when' could vary depending on business needs, individual preferences, and collaborative requirements. Organizations need to offer synchronized in-office days to encourage meaningful collaboration. For example:

- **Fixed Hybrid Models:** Teams meet in person on certain designated days to brainstorm, align priorities, and build relationships.
- **Flexible Hybrid Models:** Employees decide when they come in, creating freedom but requiring more proactive scheduling for collaboration.

Balancing flexibility with consistency is key. While employees value autonomy, an unpredictable schedule can lead to coordination issues and missed opportunities for collaboration. Clear communication about 'Anchor Days' or priority in-office times helps address this challenge.

## Finally, How Should Work Be Managed Across Locations?

Effective hybrid work management hinges on creating seamless workflows that allow employees to be productive regardless of where they work. This requires more than just setting policies; it involves fostering a culture that prioritizes trust and communication and results over physical presence.

- **Set Expectations Around Communication:** Clearly define when and how teams should communicate, whether through synchronous tools (like video calls) or asynchronous channels (like email or shared documents).
- **Establish Performance Metrics:** Focus on outcome-based goals rather than hours spent working, which helps younger employees (Millennials, Gen Z) who thrive with autonomy.
- **Promote Well-being:** Encourage employees to set boundaries between work and personal life, reducing the risk of burnout– a common issue in hybrid environments.
- **Provide Tech Support and Training:** Ensure employees across generations are comfortable with digital tools. Boomers and Gen X may need more support to adapt to

new platforms, while Millennials and Gen Z might benefit from productivity tips.

Building trust is essential for hybrid work. Managers should avoid micromanaging remote employees and instead focus on frequent check-ins, coaching, and clear deliverables to foster accountability.

## Toward a Balanced Hybrid Culture

Developing healthy hybrid practices is about balancing flexibility with structure, allowing Multi-Gen employees to choose where and when they work while providing the tools, trust, and clarity needed to succeed. By thoughtfully addressing the who, when, and how of hybrid work, organizations can create a model that caters to generational needs and ensures long-term engagement and productivity.

**More Examples**

**1. Citi**: Financial services traditionally value in-person work due to the nature of client-facing roles and a preference for fostering teamwork through close collaboration.

**Approach**: Citi has introduced a '3/2' hybrid model – three days in the office and two days remote –for most employees. This approach is structured and appealing to Baby Boomers and Gen Xers who prefer predictable schedules and in-office days. However, it still provides Millennials and Gen Z with the flexibility to work remotely part of the week, balancing autonomy and professional growth opportunities.

**Generational Impact**: The structured flexibility has been effective in balancing the needs of Boomers, who value face-to-face interactions, and Millennials and Gen Z, who seek flexibility and a sense of control over their work environments.

**2. Microsoft:** The large tech company with a workforce that spans multiple generations and emphasizes innovation and collaboration.

**Approach**: Microsoft adopted a 'hybrid workplace' policy allowing employees to work up to 50% of their week remotely, and those who want more flexibility can request full-time remote work with manager approval. Gen X employees appreciate the autonomy this policy allows, while Millennials and Gen Z enjoy the freedom it offers without sacrificing team-based innovation, as there are opportunities for regular collaboration.

**Generational Impact**: This approach acknowledges Gen Z's and Millennials' strong preferences for flexibility and purpose-driven work while also giving Boomers and Gen X opportunities for in-person mentoring and cross-generational knowledge sharing.

**3. HubSpot:** A SaaS company with a younger, tech-savvy workforce, it has a culture that emphasizes flexibility, autonomy, and employee well-being.

**Approach**: HubSpot introduced a 'choose your own adventure' hybrid model, where employees can decide to work in the office, at home, or in a hybrid arrangement based on personal preference and role needs. Millennials and Gen Z employees appreciate the high level of flexibility, allowing them to work from anywhere, while Gen X and Boomer employees can select options that support in-office days for team interactions.

**Generational Impact**: HubSpot's model especially resonates with Gen Z and Millennials, who value freedom and flexibility but also appreciate having options that cater to their needs. This autonomy has fostered strong employee satisfaction across generations.

**4. PwC (PricewaterhouseCoopers):** Consulting firms have traditionally required substantial face-to-face time for client interactions, yet PwC is pioneering hybrid work solutions in consulting.

**Approach**: PwC allows its US employees to work virtually and set their schedules. Employees can work entirely remotely, with the option to come to the office as needed. This flexibility appeals to Millennials and Gen Z, who are accustomed to digital work and prefer flexibility. For those seeking structure, like Boomers, PwC provides options for designated office days and hybrid workspaces for client meetings.

**Generational Impact**: This policy is particularly attractive to Gen Z and Millennials, aligning with their preference for remote work and autonomy while providing Baby Boomers with the option to engage more traditionally if desired.

**5. Ford Motor Company:** In a legacy automotive manufacturing environment, where in-person work has been the standard, Ford has needed to balance factory-based roles with corporate functions.

**Hybrid Approach**: Ford adopted a flexible hybrid model for office-based employees, where teams can decide collectively when to work in the office versus remotely. This team-based approach allows for personalized schedules while fostering collaborative days that Boomers and Gen X prefer for team-building. Millennials and Gen Z employees appreciate the flexibility, especially as they value work-life balance and tech-forward solutions.

**Generational Impact**: This team-based hybrid policy provides structure for Baby Boomers and Gen X, who value in-person days for cohesion, while also offering flexibility for Millennials and Gen Z, who prefer a balance that accommodates personal needs.

**6. Spotify**: As a company that attracts a younger workforce and places emphasis on creativity and innovation, Spotify adopted a 'work from anywhere' policy to boost flexibility and employee well-being.

**Approach**: Spotify allows all employees to work remotely or in-office based on their preferences, aligning particularly well with Millennial and Gen Z values of autonomy, flexibility, and inclusivity. For those who enjoy collaborative, in-person environments, Spotify's offices offer spaces designed to encourage spontaneous creativity and networking.

**Generational Impact**: The freedom to choose any work environment works well for Millennials and Gen Z, who are often more comfortable with asynchronous communication and remote technology. Meanwhile, Boomers and Gen Xers who prefer face-to-face opportunities still have access to in-office work, blending autonomy with social engagement.

These examples demonstrate that generational preferences in hybrid models can coexist effectively when companies offer choice and flexibility. Tailoring hybrid policies with generational needs in mind enables companies to support well-rounded work environments, increasing employee satisfaction, retention, and productivity across the generational spectrum.

**Run this quiz to find out if there is a 'generational preference' for the workplace in your organization.**

---

1. Which generation in your firm prefers structured, face-to-face collaboration for brainstorming sessions?
   A) Boomers
   B) Gen X
   C) Millennials
   D) Gen Z
2. When setting up hybrid meeting formats, which generation in your company prefers asynchronous options (e.g., recorded videos)?
   A) Boomers
   B) Gen X
   C) Millennials
   D) Gen Z
3. What's the biggest challenge for Gen Z in a remote-first hybrid model?
   A) Lack of access to technology
   B) Difficulty finding meaning in work
   C) Limited opportunities for mentorship and in-person learning
   D) Preference for rigid 9-to-5 structures
   E) None of the above
4. Which generation in your firm is most comfortable with blurred lines between personal and professional life and managing work?
   A) Boomers

B) Gen X
C) Millennials
D) Gen Z

5. In terms of performance metrics, which approach would your managers most likely prefer?
   A) Hours spent working
   B) Output and results
   C) Real-time feedback from managers
   D) Peer feedback and collaborative assessments

6. What type of technology support is most effective in your firm for bridging generational differences in hybrid workplaces?
   A) Extensive onboarding only for new hires
   B) Regular cross-generational tech training and support
   C) Relying on employees to learn tools independently
   D) Limiting new technology to minimize confusion

7. What is your strategy to engage employees in a hybrid model?
   A) Offering career growth through continuous learning programs
   B) Hosting virtual happy hours and social events
   C) Providing mentorship opportunities with senior leaders
   D) Emphasizing financial rewards and benefits

8. Which model of hybrid work is appealing to your Millennials and Gen Z employees?
   A) Office-first model with mandatory attendance
   B) Fixed hybrid model with scheduled office days

C) Remote-first with occasional in-person meetups
D) Fully remote with no physical office presence

You decide the 'CORRECT' answer as each of the responses you give will be contextual to your situation, so it will vary from organization to organization. Hopefully, your 'As Is State' is matching your 'Desired State.'

CHAPTER 3

# Emails, Emojis and Everything in Between: Aligning Generational Communication

> 'The single biggest problem in communication is the illusion that it has taken place.'
>
> —George Bernard Shaw

I was invited to speak at a large conference in July 2023. It was a GCC (Global Capability Center, a captive IT unit) of a global automaker. There were about 500 attendees, comprising all four generations at the workplace, but Gen Ys and Zs made up close to 50% of that audience. One of their themes was **'Leading and Managing a Multi-Generational Workforce.'** It was structured in a Q&A format, and one of their senior business leaders and head of learning had identified several issues on the topic on which they wanted my perspective.

Their opening question to me was on how to 'communicate' effectively among generations. In response to the question, I asked what the typical challenges were, and we heard the following story:

## Client Story

Veena was in back-to-back meetings. It was a typical Monday for her. The new week started with many important client calls, deliverables and internal team meetings. One such important client meeting was with Xtronics. It was a closing meeting, and the client was going to discuss the final 'finishing formalities' before hiring (VTIS) for their digital transformation work.

Xtronics CEO / CTO and Project Manager were at the meeting. On the VTIS side, it was Veena, Kusum and Hitesh (the college graduate) who was doing his first year with VTIS. The meeting was scheduled for 3:00 PM. Both Veena and Kusum had back-to-back meetings from the morning and were running behind (as is common) with global colleagues and time zones.

Veena knew that she would not make the 3:00 PM meeting on time and did not have a chance to connect with Kusum, who was also in back-to-back meetings. The team had met on Friday to review everything and knew the 'closing' pitch for Xtronics. However, due to the delayed schedule she requested her new hire Hitesh to intimate the client that the meeting may be 15 minutes behind schedule. She wanted Hitesh to inform the client so there were no surprises. Hitesh knew Veena was busy and said he would convey this to the client team.

Hitesh, who was recently hired, had undergone the VTIS orientation and had learned all about the company values, policies, and benefits.

At 3:15 PM Veena and Kusum finally able to catch their breath and attend the closing meeting with Xtronics. To her surprise the Xtronics team had been on the call since 3:00 PM and seemed quite visibly upset.

Upon learning about this, she asked Hitesh if he had relayed the message. Hitesh confirmed and indicated that he had sent a WhatsApp message and a Slack post to the Xtronics team. The Xtronics team had not received any prior messages from Veena on WhatsApp and had not read Hitesh's note. What should Veena do?

## Communication in a Multi-Gen Workforce

Many years ago, at my previous firm, we hosted a 'Friends Day' event in Delhi, designed to show appreciation for current clients in the city by bringing thought leaders from our side and then organizing a talk about a contemporary topic of leadership. The event was also extended to friends of our clients who could bring in HR and business colleagues from different firms to give them a feel of our work and offerings.

This kind of event required a fair bit of planning, especially when it came to the alignment of multiple stakeholders and their needs. We had to think of the speakers' dates, the venue, timings, logistics, and, most importantly, the marketing to ensure we had sufficient footfalls.

Our team was a classic Multi-Gen team. The Boomer in our team, also the head of the region, preferred detailed face-to-face meetings. She would call for a series of formal meetings to discuss the event's agenda, vendor contracts, guest list and so on and ask everyone to contribute verbally during these meetings for a thorough discussion.

The two Gen Xers' focus was on efficiency and preferred emails for updates and decision-making. It was about concise emails summarizing the meeting outcomes, deadlines, and next steps. Most communication was direct, occasionally followed up with a quick phone call to ensure everyone was on the same page.

However, the team comprised a larger number of Gen Ys and Zs. They suggested creating a shared online document where the team could collaborate in real-time. They preferred to communicate through instant messaging for quick questions and updates. They wanted the flexibility to work on the event details asynchronously and assumed everyone was comfortable with digital tools.

Some suggested using a project management app to streamline tasks and timelines, using short video messages to share creative ideas, and setting up a group chat for instant communication. They preferred the more informal, digital-first communication – visual content over long emails or meetings.

As the team worked on planning the event, differences in communication styles became apparent, but not to the point where it stopped progress on our work. Upon completion, however, we could see that there was a clear preference for communication styles by generations.

## Impact of Technology on Communications

The rapid advancement of technology has significantly altered the way we communicate in the workplace. Baby Boomers and Gen X, who adapted to digital tools later in their careers, may still prefer traditional communication methods or require more time to adjust to new platforms. Conversely, Millennials and Gen Z, who have grown up with the internet and smartphones, are adept at using a wide array of digital tools for communication, from video conferencing to collaborative apps. This generational divide in technological fluency can lead to miscommunication or frustration if not appropriately managed.

## Informal Versus Formal and Non-Verbal Communication

The level of formality in communication also often varies across generations, influenced by workplace culture and societal expectations. Baby Boomers, who were accustomed to more hierarchical and formal workplace structures, may prefer a professional tone in emails and meetings. Generation X, while slightly more relaxed, still values clear and structured communication. In contrast, Millennials and Gen Z often favor a more informal, conversational style, reflecting the flatter organizational structures and collaborative work environments they are accustomed to. I recall seeing this in our email exchanges with my team. I would always address my colleagues with 'Dear or Hi' salutations, and my young team would either text or write emails with 'Hey Nikhil,' not worrying too much about the formal hierarchical structure.

> Baby Boomers, who were accustomed to more hierarchical and formal workplace structures, may prefer a professional tone in emails and meetings. Generation X, while slightly more relaxed, still values clear and structured communication. In contrast, Millennials and Gen Z often favor a more informal, conversational style, reflecting the flatter organizational structures and collaborative work environments they are accustomed to.

Also, non-verbal communication, such as body language, eye contact, and facial expressions, can vary widely across generations and can be a significant source of misunderstanding. Baby Boomers and Generation X may place a higher value on traditional non-verbal cues, such as maintaining eye contact and using formal body language in professional settings. Meanwhile, Millennials and Gen Z, who are more accustomed to digital communication, might be less attuned to these cues or interpret them differently.

## Conflict and Feedback Styles

Generational differences in communication styles can also sometimes lead to conflicts in the workplace, especially when these differences are not understood or respected. Baby Boomers and Generation X may prefer to address conflicts directly and in person, often valuing a straightforward approach. In contrast, Millennials and Gen Z might opt for more indirect methods, such as using digital communication to address issues, or they might avoid conflict altogether, preferring to resolve issues collaboratively rather than confrontationally.

## Client Story:

For more than 10 years, I used to conduct a team workshop for a reputed B-School in Singapore. It was a medical program that was designed to allow students to work in teams and be evaluated as a team. So, it did not matter if you were brilliant individually because that only contributed to 50% of your grade weightage. The other 50% came from how the team performed collectively as a unit. This special program was designed to help transition students to the real-world dynamics of working in a team when they enter the workplace in a hospital. At that time, doctors had the advantage of working with individuals across different age groups and roles, including administrators, nurses, health officials, and patients. We would conclude our workshop with a 'Team Charter' of how the team would operate. These were the explicit and implicit rules of the team. However, as time progressed teams would inevitably have conflicts.

The designers for the program would do a 'Team Check-In' meeting with me about one semester into the process. This was to get a pulse of the team and their progress. A survey would be conducted where people could make comments on how they were working with each other. During these meetings I often witnessed non-verbal cues of a problem within a team such as a sense of discomfort among members when a conflict was present. No one was willing to share in the open, and often negative feedback about a colleague was shared anonymously through the online survey. While this wasn't true of everyone, a majority preferred this method. Then I would facilitate a conversation and bring the issues to the table. This was indicative of their method of communicating.

Feedback, therefore, is also a crucial component of workplace communication, and different generations have varying expectations and preferences for how it should be delivered. Boomers and Gen X, who grew up in more hierarchical structures, may expect formal, less frequent feedback, often delivered in one-on-one settings. Millennials and Gen Z, however, tend to prefer more immediate, continuous feedback, often in real-time and in a more informal manner, such as through quick check-ins or digital platforms. Many companies have ditched traditional annual appraisal or bi-annual formal structure of employee performance/feedback.

Here are some examples of what companies are doing.

**Adobe**: Adobe was one of the pioneers in ditching annual performance reviews in favor of its 'Check-In' system. This approach encourages continuous feedback throughout the year, allowing managers and employees to have regular conversations about performance, development, and goals.

**Accenture**: Accenture transitioned to a real-time feedback system where employees receive ongoing input on their performance. This shift is designed to promote more dynamic discussions and help employees make immediate improvements rather than waiting for annual reviews.

**Microsoft**: Microsoft moved away from traditional performance reviews in favor of a more flexible feedback approach.

**General Electric**: GE replaced its annual appraisal system with a mobile app-based system called 'Performance Development,' which allows for continuous, real-time feedback.

**Deloitte**: Deloitte implemented a new performance management system that includes weekly check-ins between team leaders and employees. The goal is to provide immediate feedback and focus on forward-looking development rather than past performance.

## Bridging Communication Gaps:

These varying preferences we discussed above can create challenges in a multi-generational workforce, where a one-size-fits-all approach to communication may not be effective.

Bridging the communication gaps between generations requires a deliberate and inclusive approach. Organizations can benefit from creating opportunities for cross-generational interactions, such as mentoring programs where younger employees can share their digital expertise while learning from the experience and wisdom of older colleagues.

It's important to establish clear communication guidelines that respect all team members' preferences while maintaining professionalism. Encouraging an open dialogue about these differences can also help create a more inclusive and understanding work environment. Promoting an environment of respect and curiosity, where employees are encouraged to ask questions and learn about each other's communication preferences, can help to break down barriers.

In the end, leadership plays a crucial role in this process by modelling inclusive communication behaviors and ensuring that the workplace culture supports diverse communication styles. This will involve implementing flexible communication strategies based on generational differences and using a variety of communication platforms to ensure that everyone's preferences are accommodated.

Here is a chart I prepared for a conference in which I spoke in 2022 on how companies can use a Comms Guideline to indicate which medium is to be used when and the respective response times.

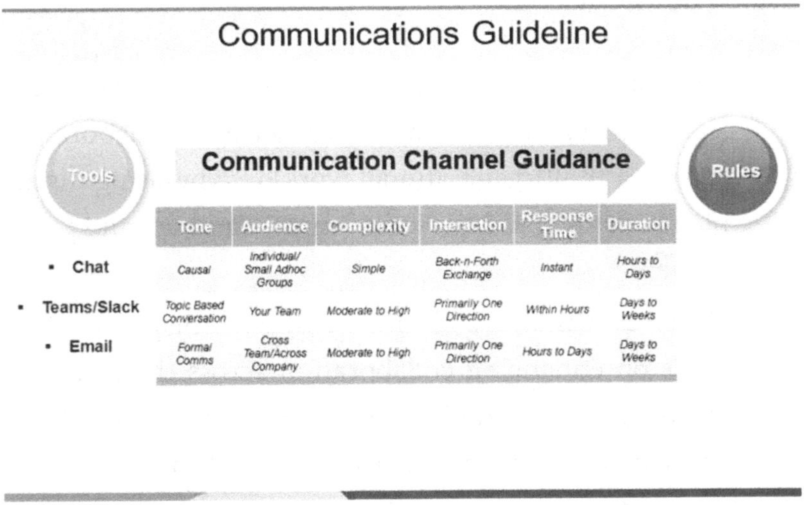


Fig 3.0 Communication Guide with Tools and their Utility

**Examples**: Here are examples of companies using specific initiatives and various communication tools to bridge generational gaps, ensuring that all employees can connect and collaborate effectively regardless of age or preferred communication style.

In many instances, younger employees might lead digital initiatives, helping to bridge the gap by enabling older employees to learn in a peer-supported environment. Tools like video conferencing are used for more personal interactions, instant messaging for quick exchanges and internal social networks for informal communication and idea sharing among employees. Finally, companies also run workshops to help employees understand the benefits and best practices of each platform, ensuring that no one is left behind in the digital transformation.

1. **Siemens:** The company's 'Next Work' initiative is designed to enhance communication and collaboration among a multi-generational workforce by using digital platforms such as Microsoft Teams, Yammer, and Cisco Webex.
2. **Unilever**: Unilever's 'Connected 4 Growth' program focuses on enhancing collaboration across the company by using various digital tools, including Trello, Slack, and video conferencing platforms like Zoom.
3. **General Electric (GE):** GE launched a comprehensive 'Digital Workplace Transformation' initiative, which includes the deployment of various communication tools like Microsoft Teams, Yammer, and Workplace by Facebook.
4. **Deloitte:** Deloitte's 'Workplace of the Future' program includes the adoption of a variety of communication platforms, including Skype for Business, Yammer, and Microsoft Teams, to facilitate communication across different generations.
5. **IBM:** IBM's 'Digital Mentor' program pairs employees from different generations to learn from each other's strengths, particularly in using digital communication

tools. (Watson Workspace is integrated into other platforms.)

6. **Ford Motor Company:** Ford's 'Smart Mobility' initiative includes the deployment of digital communication tools like Microsoft Teams, Zoom, and an internal social network to foster collaboration among its diverse workforce.
7. **Coca-Cola:** Coca-Cola's 'Coke One North America' (CONA) IT platform integrates various communication and collaboration tools, including Microsoft 365 and SharePoint, to streamline operations and communication across its workforce.
8. **Nestlé:** Nestlé's 'Project Shield' is a cybersecurity initiative that also emphasizes the importance of secure communication across different generations within the company.
9. **Procter & Gamble (P&G):** P&G has implemented a 'Digital Skills Training' initiative that focuses on enhancing digital literacy across all generations within the company.
10. **AT&T:** AT&T's 'Digital You' program is designed to help employees and customers across generations improve their digital literacy, including the use of various communication platforms.

CHAPTER 4

# Ageism: The Silent Discriminator of Generations. It Cuts Both Ways

'Age is how we measure the passage of time, not the value of a person.'

—Ellen Goodman

## Personal Story

My very first job out of college was in East Lansing, Michigan, doing financial sales. We were four graduates recruited from the same class and hired by a large financial advisory firm. Anyone wanting to sell securities has to obtain a Series-7 Securities License. This license allows you to buy and sell on behalf of clients and give advice on financial products. In financial sales, the Series 7 is often the first round of eliminator. In many firms, those who don't clear this exam are automatically weeded out of the recruiting process. A stint in financial sales will generally involve building a personal practice for clients based on selling financial products: mutual funds, annuities, stocks, bonds, derivatives, and so on. It is a tough grind. There is evidence of more people quitting within the first year itself, given the sheer perseverance needed to make it through a sales career. As with any sales role this form of selling requires you to take rejections on the chin and show resilience. To succeed, you either come with a great book of contacts who are willing to give you some business in the early years of your practice or you find clients who will do that.

For us, we were a fee-based firm which means we would charge the clients a fee first for designing a financial plan which would lay out the roadmap to achieving their financial goals. This was done based on understanding their goals, age, risk appetite, tax brackets, etc. Based on what the client decided to implement we would then recommend the necessary products. So, in some sense, not recommending just products that are often driven only by sales commissions a fee first would create some objectivity.

A typical day would look like this: Start with sales training from 8:00 AM to 12:00 PM. The afternoon segment (1:00 to 5:00 pm) would generally be when young advisors shadowed experienced Financial Advisors in client meetings. They were primarily there to observe and learn. It could be an intro client meeting, data collection or closing a sales pitch meeting. The evenings (6:00 to 8:00 PM) would be cold calling clients or attending client meetings. The cold calling was kept for the evening because this is when most prospects or existing clients would come home from work, and it was a good time to connect and understand their needs. This was the time when we did not have any social media. This would be done for several hours in the evening, before we took stock of how it went. How many prospects were contacted? How many converted, and how the sales pipeline looked for the week? So, a typical day would start at 8:00 AM and end no earlier than 9:00 PM.

All of the new graduates had to go through this intense routine throughout the first year. During this year we got a salary as well. In a way, it was the company's way of investing in us and giving us a chance to learn the business. Depending upon your effort and promise, you were then sent to a corporate learning center at the end of the year for an all-paid two-week training which really gave you great exposure to the best in the game in the financial advisory business. After completing this training, we would enter our second year when the salary would stop completely, and you only worked on commissions and took home what you sold.

Our office was in the company's number one sales-producing region for more than 20 years. Some of the highest-producing advisors were present, and it was often said, 'If you could survive the pressures of this region, you could make it anywhere.'

We had a manager with about 10 years of experience in the field and a district manager who was the manager's manager who was much more senior and oversaw multiple regional offices.

After about one year into the business, our office hired Alan, perhaps in his 60s, to join our group. He had been a life insurance agent for most of his life and now found himself selling financial plans. It was a difficult transition. Many of his old clients learned about this but resisted paying fees. Alan came in with great enthusiasm and was convinced that 'fee-based' planning was something no one did and that we were ahead of our time and our competitors.

However, anyone who joined this firm, irrespective of their level of experience, had to principally change their way of selling (i.e., do a financial plan and only then talk about products). Everyone had to go through a rigorous routine and create a successful practice through the 'advisory' philosophy of selling. Those who showed promise were kept or eventually booted out. Alan too had to go through the same daily schedule as we did. Over time, we saw that it was becoming hard for him to adjust to the long hours and the new way of selling. There were questions about his contribution to bringing clients for his practice and the assets for the office. Given all this, after 6 months or so, there were also murmurs about whether the company should send him to the corporate learning training. They also saw a much shorter runway from him (or foreseeing him retiring soon) as they were trying to build the next cadre of advisors for the office. Alan was slowly distanced from conversations, meetings, and training support, which was slowly declining. In the next two months, Alan eventually saw that the results were not quite what he would have liked, and his enthusiasm was waning. He stayed for another two months and then quit! Most importantly, given his age and the learning curve he took to adapt to the new ways of selling, the company felt this was for the best. In many large firms, employees are put through a PIP (Personal Improvement Plan) to give them time to implement constructive feedback, after which if nothing changes, they are let go. In this case, it was felt that 'let him bow out on his own, and let's turn the focus on investing and developing younger talent.'

## What Is Ageism and Why Is it Important to Address it at Work?

Ageism refers to stereotypes (how we think), prejudice (how we feel) and discrimination (how we act) towards others or oneself based on age.

Ageism affects everyone. Children as young as four years old become aware of their culture's age stereotypes. From that age onward they internalize and use these stereotypes to guide their feelings and behavior toward people of different ages. They also draw on culture's age stereotypes to perceive and understand themselves, which can result in self-directed ageism at any age. Ageism intersects and exacerbates other forms of disadvantage, including those related to race, gender and disability.

Age bias more commonly involves discrimination against older employees. However, younger employees, too, can experience ageism as well.

The common stereotypes about older employees include:

- Resistant to learning new approaches.
- They are not tech-savvy.
- They are less healthy as compared with younger workers.
- They can be slower than younger employees, which means that they are less productive.

There are also the stereotypes that younger workers experience to provide a more complete picture:

- Younger employees are lazier.
- They can be less motivated and unreliable when it comes to work.
- They can be arrogant.
- They are not very loyal to the employer.

Much of my work involves working with High Potential Managers, meaning promising mid-career leaders are getting ready for senior leader roles and experienced line managers are being groomed for middle manager positions. Inevitably, in these programs, we do 360° diagnostic assessments. This means we speak to HR and learning colleagues – the target participant's bosses, their direct reports (or subordinates), peers and participants themselves – to get a feel for the learning gaps. This gives us a well-rounded view of the positives and areas of improvement from stakeholders, and we can juxtapose one's own assessment vis-à-vis the bosses' and direct reports. In these conversations, we learn from Gen Zs about their boss's management style and some of the ageism biases they experience. I have observed this across various industries, from manufacturing to consulting, and in roles ranging from client-facing to support functions. All of this has a direct bearing on morale, retention and engagement.

I have listed below first the eight most common reverse ageism biases (in the form of short stories and their impact) that young employees have shared.

**1. Hiring Bias**

A talented 28-year-old software engineer applies for a senior developer position at a well-known tech startup. During the interview process, she impresses the panel with her extensive knowledge and innovative ideas. However, the hiring manager dismisses her abilities, saying, 'You're very young to be applying for a senior role. We usually look for someone with more "life experience".'

Despite her qualifications and experience, the person is passed over for the role, which is given to an older candidate with less relevant experience but who is perceived as more mature. This can make the employee feel discouraged and begin to doubt their skills, not because of their actual abilities but because of the bias against age.

**2. Undermining Authority**

A 30-year-old financial analyst is promoted to a management position in a large corporation. He is enthusiastic about bringing fresh ideas and a modern approach to the team. However, his older colleagues often undermine his authority, making comments like, 'What can he teach us? He's just a kid.'

During meetings, his suggestions are frequently dismissed without consideration, and he is excluded from important discussions. His colleagues assume that his age makes him less capable of leading the team effectively. Despite his efforts to prove himself, he faces constant resistance, leading to frustration and decreased morale.

**3. Disregarding Contributions**

A 25-year-old social worker joins a nonprofit organization dedicated to helping at-risk youth. She has a master's degree in social work and several years of relevant experience. Emma is passionate about her work and brings innovative strategies to the table.

However, her older colleagues and supervisors often overlook her contributions, attributing her ideas to her 'lack of experience.' One day, during a staff meeting, she proposes a new outreach program that could significantly benefit their target community. Her supervisor responds, 'You have great enthusiasm, but maybe we should stick to traditional methods. You're still new to this field.' Her innovative approach is dismissed because of her age, causing her to feel undervalued and discouraged.

**4. Promotion Bias / Leadership Roles**

A 26-year-old marketing specialist has been working at a marketing agency for four years. He has consistently delivered outstanding results, leading successful campaigns that significantly increased the company's revenue. When a senior marketing manager position opens up, Vikas applies for it, confident in his track record and abilities.

However, during the promotion evaluation, the senior executives express concerns about Vikas's age, saying, 'He's too young to handle the pressures of a senior role. We need someone with more years under their belt.' Despite his proven competence, the promotion is given to an older colleague with fewer accomplishments but more years of experience.

**5. Client Trust Issues**

A 29-year-old lawyer works at a prestigious law firm. She has successfully handled many high-profile cases and has a solid reputation among her peers. However, she often encounters clients who doubt her capabilities solely based on her age. One client explicitly requests a different lawyer, saying, 'I want someone who has been practicing for at least 20 years. I don't trust someone so young with my case.' Her age becomes a barrier to her professional relationships and client trust despite her excellent legal skills and track record.

**6. Colleague Resentment**

A 31-year-old management consultant quickly rises through the ranks at his consulting firm due to his innovative problem-solving skills and strong client relationships. However, his rapid advancement sparks resentment among older colleagues who have been with the firm longer but have not advanced as quickly. They make comments like, 'He must be a favorite of the bosses because there's no way someone his age could achieve this on merit alone.'

The employee's accomplishments are unfairly attributed to favoritism rather than his hard work and talent, causing tension and undermining his professional achievements.

**7. Training Opportunities**

A 24-year-old assistant store manager at a major retail chain is eager to attend an advanced leadership training program offered by the company. She has demonstrated exceptional leadership skills and consistently exceeds performance targets. However, her request to participate in the program is denied, with her supervisor stating, 'You have plenty of time to develop your career. Let's give this opportunity to someone who's been with us longer.' The employee feels that her professional growth is being stunted because of her age, even though she has proven her potential and readiness for further development.

**8. Recognition and Awards**

A 29-year-old researcher makes a significant breakthrough in his field and submits his findings to a prestigious scientific journal. Despite the high quality and originality of his work, the review committee is hesitant to award him the recognition he deserves, questioning, 'Can someone so young truly make such a significant contribution?' The employee's age leads to skepticism about his capabilities, delaying the publication of his research and the recognition of his contributions to the field.

Now, let's turn our focus to a few more stories of ageism biases as they relate to older employees. There are eight common biases that I share below.

**1. Recruiting Only Young People (Age Bias)**

A pharmaceutical company purposefully refused to hire older workers due to age. The company began by hiring more senior candidates and recruiting more Millennials to build a more age-balanced workforce.

More than a third of those over 50 feel disadvantaged when applying for jobs. It's not uncommon for this feeling to start with a job advert. It might contain language that has younger connotations, such as 'looking for a recent graduate' and/or 'someone who's dynamic and innovative.' Though people over 50 are capable of meeting these criteria, the societal connotations can hint that a company is looking for a younger candidate, which can be off-putting for older workers. Many people in their 50s looking to transition into roles that don't directly align with their experience and skill level may also be branded by employers as 'overqualified' and overlooked as a result. Or they may not be chosen for progressive roles due to the incorrect assumption that older adults have little interest in career development.

**2. Not Receiving Challenging Tasks / Assumption of Technical Incompetence**

One tactic often used by employers that aims to influence older workers to leave their jobs is through lightening their workload or not assigning them challenging tasks. Frustration can set in among older employees assigned unsatisfying tasks, making them feel useless and not valuable in their company. Consequently, the stereotypical belief that older employees are not as skillful and knowledgeable continues.

Aman is made redundant because of an alleged lack of work. However, it is revealed by prior emails among managers that there were discussions about hiring younger experts instead of Aman. Aman receives a notice of termination that makes no reference to redundancy, and later, he gets a notice that cites the downturn in the business as the cause. When Aman brings up concerns about age discrimination, the MD takes an aggressive stance. When the matter is taken to court, it is then determined the company is unable to prove redundancy or performance as grounds for termination. The age discrimination argument is supported by the email comments, which show age-based motivation.

**3. Incentivizing Retirement**

To push their older employees out, organizations may offer retirement packages. It's usually hard for older employees to turn down these incentives; if they don't, there is no guarantee that the company won't fire them. In a similar way, organizations may enact a mandatory retirement age even though mandatory retirement is only legal in certain cases and can vary from market to market. In other words, forced retirement is an involuntary process that usually occurs during downsizing, restructuring, or as a result of an employee's health problems.

John is a highly experienced engineer in his late 60s working at a manufacturing company for over three decades. He has consistently demonstrated exceptional skills and knowledge in his field and enjoys his work. However, the company's management wants to reduce labor costs and bring in younger, lower-paid employees. To achieve this, the company's management devises a strategy to encourage older employees like John to retire early. They offer an early retirement package that includes financial incentives such as a lump-sum payment and continued healthcare coverage. The company's management also starts gradually reducing John's responsibilities, removing him from high-impact projects and reallocating his tasks to younger engineers.

**4. Getting Turned Down for Promotions**

You could be turned down for promotion on many accounts.

**Gender Discrimination**: A single mother is passed up for a promotion because her boss believes she has 'too many kids' and not enough support to become a manager.

**Age Discrimination**: A 60-year-old high-performing and well-deserving worker is denied a promotion because the company fears that due to their age, they may not understand the newest technology trends.

**Pregnancy Discrimination**: A qualified pregnant worker is denied a promotion upon return from maternity leave, as their supervisor assumes they aren't available for long hours due to having a newborn.

**Racial Discrimination**: A high-performing Indian employee is passed up on a promotion for a less qualified Caucasian woman because management fears they may not 'fit in' with the all-white leadership team, given his accent and long last name.

**5. Marginalization / Isolating Old Employees**

Marginalisation is usually the result of stereotyping and happens when someone is made to feel of lesser importance than others in society. They're essentially sidelined and made to feel small. In the case of marginalisation at work, once someone has been labelled with a stereotype, they might:

- Be excluded from important meetings (such as those on tech or future strategies),
- Have their opinions and suggestions ignored,
- Be placed in roles that offer limited opportunities for growth and development,

While marginalisation can be achieved explicitly or more subtly – sometimes as the result of unconscious bias – it can be incredibly damaging, not just to an individual's confidence, self-esteem, and happiness at work but to organisations too. Companies that lose employees due to marginalisation will lack diversity. This means they'll have a much narrower range of ideas and perspectives, making evolution more difficult, especially in an ageing population.

### 6. Isolation

Employers who want to coerce older workers into leaving their jobs may push employees to the sidelines of the organization by isolating them. They may isolate these employees by excluding them from meetings, not allocating the required resources for them, and restricting their access to opportunities, services or common areas. Employers may even go one step further and ask their older employees to work remotely, or they may appoint them to a different physical location, significantly disrupting their lives. As a result of the feelings of isolation, employees may experience reluctance to contribute and participate.

Rather than firing senior nurses directly, hospital administration chooses to isolate them in order to save money. They begin by putting them on less difficult shifts and excluding them from training sessions. In addition, senior nurses are transferred to distant departments or locations, which disrupts their routines and damages their sense of belonging.

A 55-year-old nurse observes the change in treatment. She used to actively participate in quality improvement projects and serve as a mentor to newer nurses. She now feels under-appreciated and ignored, which lowers her morale and job satisfaction. She is committed to providing excellent patient care, but her isolation makes her think about quitting earlier than she had intended.

In my story, Alan, our newest employee, was slowly being isolated due to his slow transition to adjusting to a new way of selling and also his age.

**7. Going Through Layoffs**

Sarah, a 55-year-old production supervisor with 30 years of expertise, is one of the people let go. Even in roles comparable to hers, she observes that younger workers with less tenure and experience are kept on the team. The corporation includes a tiny sample of younger workers in the layoffs to minimize legal ramifications, but the majority of the staff is still older. Sarah chooses to file a lawsuit for age discrimination against the employer after noticing a pattern. She collects proof of the unfair impact on senior employees and demands compensation.

Layoffs, when they only target older employees, can be a sign of ageism in the workplace. You can prove age discrimination if you notice a pattern like this in your organization. To avoid legal repercussions, employers may include a small sample of younger employees into the mix of laid-off employees for ageism-related wrongful termination.

**8. Re-Branding Roles / Not Receiving Training Opportunities**

Employers may assume that older workers are slow to learn, and this assumption can lead to a lack of access to learning and development opportunities.

Jill is fired because of her age after refusing to retire when she turned 65. The employee's manager repeatedly asks her when she will retire. And once she tells the company that she isn't going to, they inform her that her position is being eliminated due to economic uncertainty. Less than a month later, the company hires a man in his thirties for the same position the company claims to have eliminated.

Rebranding roles in the workplace is a prime example of ageism that occurs all too often. It involves older employees being informed that their position is being phased out, only for the company to then bring in a younger individual to essentially carry out the same responsibilities, albeit under a different title.

## What Is the Impact of Ageism on the Workplace?

Ageism in the workplace can have two fundamentally detrimental effects.

The first is Organizational Performance. By perpetuating stereotypes and biases against older or younger workers, companies miss out on valuable skills, knowledge, and experience that older or younger employees bring to the table. This limits diversity of thought and hinders innovation and creativity within the organization. Ageism also undermines teamwork and collaboration by creating divisions and conflicts among different age groups.

By perpetuating stereotypes and biases against older or younger workers, companies miss out on valuable skills, knowledge, and experience that older or younger employees bring to the table. This limits diversity of thought and hinders innovation and creativity within the organization.

The second is Negative Employer Brand. Ageism in the workplace also creates a negative and hostile work environment for everyone impacted. Those affected may experience discrimination, exclusion, and unfair treatment solely based on their age. This can lead to decreased job satisfaction, lower self-esteem, and increased stress levels among older and younger workers. For all employees who experience ageism, it can limit career advancement opportunities, making them feel undervalued and marginalized. As a result, they may become disengaged and less motivated, ultimately affecting their productivity and overall contribution to the organization. This could also negatively impact the employer branding should employees voice dissatisfaction with a lack of inclusivity. Failing to tackle ageism in the workplace could also lead to potential legal repercussions if an employee decides to take legal action for discrimination.

## So, How Do We Combat Ageism at Work?

Preventing ageism in the workplace requires a proactive approach that promotes inclusivity and values employees of all age groups. By actively addressing ageism and promoting a culture of inclusivity, organizations can create a positive work environment that benefits employees and contributes to long-term success. Let's see some basic steps companies can take to overcome ageism in the system.

## Knock It Down – Talent Is Ageless

The term ageism is built on certain myths and stereotypes. However, being proactive and creating a work environment that ignores generational differences will positively impact acquisition, retention, growth, and innovation. It must start from the top, and the organizational leaders must take a clear stance against ageism. And then, it must flow down and include every organization member because collective efforts can bring holistic success. You can tap into this talent pool of older candidates who can bring experience and skills to your organization during a talent shortage. If you're currently finding it difficult to hire, this is the perfect opportunity to tap a talent pool that's too often overlooked. Below are seven simple tips on combating ageism.

**Monitor Hiring Process**: It all starts from the first step – hiring. Make sure you monitor your hiring process and check for discrimination in the hiring process. The following aspects can help you:

- Avoid using discriminatory language in your job posts.
- Avoid asking age-related questions during interviews.
- Avoid the idea of not hiring an older or younger person.

**Offer Mentorship and Training:** Host training sessions and accommodate everyone, irrespective of age, to get one step closer to an ageism-free workplace. Over and above that, ensure orientation programs for new hires and leadership training for managers. Again, the aim is to minimize age-related discrimination and treat everyone equally. Get your seasoned employees involved in training the organization's young minds to make things more favorable. This will add to their job role and their worth for the organization.

**Engage In Dialogue with Employees:** Give your employees an environment that supports open conversations and let them discuss their issues. Cultivate open lines of communication to combat age discrimination by breaking generational gaps. Additionally, this will help you acknowledge the myths and internalize stereotypes and decide on a collective action to end discrimination.

For organizations across the globe, tapping the potential of all employees, irrespective of age, always bears fruit. Therefore, encouraging healthy personal and professional conversations will help create a world for all ages.

**Devise Flexible Rules for Retirement:** The corporate world has a notion about the age that considers a person ready for retirement. However, forcing someone directly or indirectly not to take up a particular job or quit isn't ethical. In fact, you should be more open to hiring or retaining physically fit and enthusiastic professionals to work.

Your organization must have flexible retirement plans and offer opportunities to all, whether they are 20 years of age or 60! Make room for open conversation and ask your veteran employees when and how they wish to retire.

## Don't Be Manipulative or Calculative

Approaching layoffs based on age or pay is a bad idea. Unarguably, an experienced employee will always get a higher income than others because of accumulated years of experience. Therefore, targeting pay as the reason for layoffs will damage employee morale and productivity.

Organizations and their hiring managers should refrain from pushing experienced workers to exit of their own volition. Avoid being manipulative by excluding them from important meetings or finding faults with their work.

## Have Policies and Enforce Them

Put policies in place and ensure their implementation. Unarguably, it is not enough to just have policies. Their enforcement is equally vital to eliminate ageism. You must inform everyone in the organization— especially new hires. The policy must set out the non-tolerance of discrimination based on age.

Include seniors, managers, and HR personnel for enforcing policies effectively. And when employees witness senior-level workforce practicing what they preach, policies are implemented successfully.

## Employ a Multi-Generational Workforce

Finally, aim to build a culture of diversity and inclusion to drive business growth. Simply put, employing multi-generational professionals will make cross-generational learning a part of your company's culture. Experienced employees can impart their years of knowledge to the younger minds and receive tech knowledge from them.

Once you succeed at it, nothing can stop your organization from becoming an ageism-free entity. The only key is to keep sticking to the idea of valuing mature employees and not discriminating against them.

Here are some examples of what some companies are doing to address ageism:

**For Older Employees**

1. **IBM**: IBM launched the 'New-Collar Jobs' initiative, focusing on skills over age or traditional credentials, ensuring that employees of all ages are included in their workforce transformation.
2. **PwC**: PwC's 'Golden Age Index' promotes the economic case for older workers, and internally, they've implemented programs to reskill older employees, ensuring they remain competitive in the job market.
3. **BMW**: BMW redesigned its assembly lines to accommodate older workers, incorporating ergonomic improvements and flexible workstations, which improved productivity and job satisfaction across all age groups.
4. **Procter & Gamble**: P&G's 'Age Diversity Program' actively recruits and retains older employees by offering flexible working arrangements and opportunities for continuous learning, ensuring that age diversity is valued and leveraged within the company.
5. **Cigna**: Cigna's 'Age-Friendly Care' program trains employees across generations to work together in delivering healthcare services, emphasizing the value of diverse perspectives and experiences.
6. **Intel**: Intel's 'Encore Fellowships' program helps retirees transition into social-purpose roles, allowing them to apply their expertise in meaningful ways post-retire-

ment while promoting age diversity within the workforce.

7. **Home Depot**: Home Depot actively recruits retirees and offers flexible part-time positions, recognizing the value of their experience and customer service skills.
8. **Barclays**: Barclays launched the 'Bolder Apprentices' program aimed at individuals over 50, providing opportunities for career changes or re-entry into the workforce with training and support.

**For Younger Employees**

9. **Deloitte**: Deloitte implemented a 'Reverse Mentoring' program where younger employees mentor senior leaders on digital skills and new trends, promoting mutual respect and breaking down age-related stereotypes.
10. **Unilever**: Unilever has introduced initiatives to ensure younger employees have a voice in decision-making processes, encouraging intergenerational collaboration and creating leadership opportunities for younger talent.
11. **Cisco**: Cisco's 'Early-in-Career Network' provides young employees with mentoring, leadership development programs, and opportunities to participate in high-impact projects, ensuring they are not sidelined due to their age.
12. **Google**: Google's 'Project Oxygen' identified that managers needed to support the career development of younger employees, leading to initiatives that focus on

nurturing young talent and ensuring they have clear pathways to advancement.

13. **Accenture**: Accenture's 'Future Talent Program' focuses on integrating younger employees into leadership roles through training, mentoring, and accelerated career paths, ensuring they are not overlooked due to their age.
14. **SAP**: SAP has developed a 'Next-Gen Leaders Program' that offers young professionals fast-tracked leadership development, fostering an inclusive culture where young talent is recognized and nurtured.

## Personal Reflection Sheet

---

### (Multi-generation and Ageism)

What (if any) are some of the ageism discriminations you have seen in your career and organizations?

______________________________________________

______________________________________________

______________________________________________

______________________________________________

______________________________________________

______________________________________________

What approaches are you taking to overcome Ageism at your workplace?

______________________________________________

______________________________________________

______________________________________________

______________________________________________

______________________________________________

______________________________________________

______________________________________________

Please share your answer sheets and responses to www.learnwisely.in

# PART II:

## Bridging the Divide: Implementing the (POPs) Points of Parity of the Multi-Gen Work Force

CHAPTER 5

# Perceptions and Reality: Biases, Stereotypes and Meta Stereotypes

'Stereotypes are stories. They simplify complexities in people, and the real danger lies in accepting them as the full story.'

—Chimamanda Ngozi Adichie

'Labels are for filing. Labels are for clothing. Labels are not for people.'

—Martina Navratilova

## Client Story

We worked with the senior leadership of a large Non-Banking Financial Company (NBFC) that had to make a crucial decision on its branding. It was part of a family of companies of a large top brand in India. The NBFC, in its current form, had a parent company with 11 subsidiary companies which sold different products to customers under the respective individual firms; for example, a separate company for insurance, fixed instruments, equities, structured finance, etc. Many of these had joint ventures with foreign players to leverage their product portfolio. These individual brands, however, often created confusion about the parent brand, therefore, underleveraging the power of the parent company in the minds of the customers.

The company faced a key decision: Should they rebrand all subsidiaries under the parent company name for better recall (Umbrella Branding), maintain the current structure where each firm retains its identity (House of Brands), or adopt a hybrid approach, combining both strategies? The CEO had asked his senior team to think through the pros and cons of this. It was a heterogeneous class made up of many functional leaders. The idea of Umbrella Branding, while appealing to many, had its downstream consequences. For instance, how do we integrate the IT systems of 11 subsidiary firms? How do they cross-train agents on other products? How do they create an equitable commission structure for selling? What about integrating culture, job positions, titles, salaries and so on? We conducted a day's session on decision and behavioral biases. At the end of the day, the CEO asked which option would make the most sense. No one spoke. After a long silence, the CEO said it would make sense to do an Umbrella Branding. Guess what happened shortly after? The entire class started agreeing to this one by one, even though they had just discussed the challenges of integrating firms. At the conclusion of the workshop, we pulled the CEO over to say that everyone was feeling a bit overpowered by his presence and agreed to his decision out of fear of disagreement and respect for hierarchy.

This is an example of 'Group Think' bias. In this instance, most of the leaders in the classroom were from a generation which had a huge respect for the hierarchy (and also the firm's culture) of not swimming against the 'stream' which led to a Group Think response. In the subsequent batches of the same workshop, we put much younger employees through it, and when we gave them the same choice of decision, they vocally expressed their opinions on whether it aligned with the view of the CEO or not. For more batches of the older employees, the CEO then prefaced he did not have a preference and wanted to hear the team's thoughts irrespective of whether it matched with his own decision. This is when people openly shared their hopes and fears for this initiative.

In the above story, the 'Group Think' bias occurred as leaders prioritized consensus over critical thinking in a group, suppressing dissenting opinions to maintain harmony. This can lead to poor decision-making and a lack of innovation. While Group Think is a social bias one can see how different generations responded in the same situation.

## Understanding Our Biases (System 1 and System 2 Thinking)

A bias is a preconceived notion or inclination that affects judgment, often without conscious or unconscious awareness. It is generally shaped by personal experiences, cultural influences, or societal norms. So, how does a bias occur? Let's understand briefly the neuroscience behind it. The human brain receives lots of information through which it has to make decisions. Because of the sheer amount of information coming to us, the brain tends to take shortcuts when processing information which is rooted in its need to conserve energy and respond quickly to stimuli. This is explained through the concept of **System 1 and System 2 Thinking, introduced by Daniel Kahneman.** System 1 is fast, intuitive, and automatic; it relies on mental shortcuts, or heuristics, to make quick decisions, often influenced by past experiences or emotions. For example, a manager immediately assumes that a Gen Z employee prefers text communication over in-person meetings based on the stereotype that younger generations are 'always on their phones.' This quick, automatic judgment reflects System 1 Thinking.

System 1 is fast, intuitive, and automatic; it relies on mental shortcuts, or heuristics, to make quick decisions, often influenced by past experiences or emotions.

System 2, in contrast, is slow, deliberate, and analytical, requiring effort to override the snap judgments of System 1. For example, before assigning a new project, the same manager reviews the team's past performance, considers the employee's preferred communication style based on prior feedback, and schedules a meeting to discuss options. This thoughtful, evidence-based approach is an example of System 2 Thinking.

System 2, in contrast, is slow, deliberate, and analytical, requiring effort to override the snap judgments of System 1. For example, before assigning a new project, the same manager reviews the team's past performance, considers the employee's preferred communication style based on prior feedback, and schedules a meeting to discuss options.

In a workplace, System 1 Thinking might lead to unconscious biases, such as making assumptions about a colleague based on age or stereotypes, while System 2 Thinking allows for more thoughtful, fair evaluations. In a multi-generational workplace, biases may occur when individuals make assumptions about colleagues based on their generational identity. For example, one might believe that younger employees lack commitment or that older colleagues are resistant to change. These biases often arise from stereotypes, communication gaps, or a lack of exposure to diverse perspectives. Such biases can hinder collaboration, innovation, and mutual respect in the workplace if not actively addressed. Balancing these systems is essential for mitigating bias and fostering more objective decision-making. Most managers (who are self-aware) would accept they have some form of bias in them. For those who disagree, you could do the following simple and fun test.

## Bias (Test)

---

**Example:** Let us do a quick test which proves that almost all of us have biases of some form. You can give your team the task of remembering the following 10 words (giving them 5-8 seconds). They cannot take pictures but have to memorize them. Ask them the words to confirm the list as you read them out. Try inserting the word 'sleep' about 5 or 6 words into your quiz. There is a good chance most people will say 'yes' to it. I have done this several times in my workshops, and more than 50% of the time, people fall for it. What has happened is that the brain took the shortcut in deciding. So, while sleep itself wasn't there, the brain jumps to a conclusion to say yes to sleep as everything on the list is related to sleep.

| | |
|---|---|
| Slumber | Pillow |
| Dream | Night |
| Bed | Blanket |
| Quiet | Pyjamas |
| Nap | Snooze |

Similarly, you can conduct a 'Perception Test' by asking people to see what they find in the images below. If they have seen these images before, they may say the correct answer. For those seeing for the first time, the answer will be different. For image one, you may hear either rabbit or duck. For image two, you may hear either an old lady or a young lady, and for image 3 you may hear a man playing a saxophone or a lady with a mask. For those who answered any one choice (above) try showing the image again, and they will see the other image. This shows that unless we make a conscious effort to see from the other perspective, we only see the image from one angle (or our own perspective).

Fig 5.0 Perception Test

## Biases and Impact on the Multi-Gen Workforce

There are over 180 identified behavioral biases, though the exact number can vary depending on how researchers categorise or define them. These biases are typically grouped into categories such as cognitive biases (e.g., confirmation bias, anchoring bias), social biases (e.g., Group Think, authority bias), and decision-making biases (e.g., loss aversion, overconfidence bias). While not exhaustive, this growing list highlights how human decision-making is often influenced by mental shortcuts and heuristics.

In this section, we will explore the common behavioral biases we all may fall prey to which impacts working with our colleagues. I have created a table of the different biases and their impact at the workplace but I have shared the story of Confirmation Bias which we experienced as parents for my son.

## Cognitive Biases: Confirmation Bias

When my son passed out of Grade X, he had to make a choice on which stream to choose. Will it be Science (means a career as an engineer or doctor), commerce (chartered accountant or entrepreneur) or Arts (career in Liberal Arts)? He always liked Science (especially Biology) and was also good at problem-solving. When speaking to doctors, he could see that it was a very respected profession and financially rewarding; the same for engineers and even those in commerce. There was no pressure from our end on him, and we said he was free to choose whatever he wanted. As he spoke to people in our family and friends circle, he was getting increasingly confused. In the end, we sought the school principal's counsel. She asked whether we had talked to him about the 'other perspective or the other side' for each of the careers. For medicine, generally, there are 12 years of education before you start earning; for engineers, In India, we produce more engineers, but are they 'employable?' Also, for being a chartered accountant, the exam in India is so tough that most people take a few attempts before clearing it by which time a student could be demotivated and shift his career choice into doing something else. So, the more he understood the 'other side' of each profession (effort, time, ROI, etc.), the more it helped him gain more clarity. In the end, he chose to study business with supply chain as his major.

At the workplace, we use this bias more often than we realize. For example, when we have a tough assignment or a tough client to manage, we first talk to people who will confirm our thinking that we should not take this. It could be a bad move for our careers. It will jeopardize a possible promotion, and so on. The whole purpose of speaking to those friends is that it is precisely what we want to hear. Instead, what would happen if we consciously built a habit of seeking an alternate view and seeing if there is any merit in it? Perhaps this chance of managing a tough assignment or client (if done successfully) could be an opportunity that could really put us on the 'Senior Leaders Radar'. They may see you as a high-potential leader ready to take on bigger assignments. So, the more we get into a routine of seeking another 'perspective,' the more we can open our blind spots. This is especially true when managing a Multi-Gen workforce. Rather than confirming a belief we may have about someone (an older person thinking of Gen Zs as lazy or Gen Z thinking of the older generation as resistant to change), if we consciously seek their perspective, we could potentially leverage an opportunity we may not see. Below is a table of the common biases, with examples of their impact on the workplace and how we can de-bias or overcome them.

| Type of Bias | What It Means | Impact on the Multi-Gen | Example | How to De-Biase |
|---|---|---|---|---|
| **Confirmation Bias** | Seeking information that confirms pre-existing beliefs while ignoring contradictory evidence. | Reinforces generational stereotypes, leading to misjudgements about others' skills or motivations. | A Millennial project manager assumes Baby Boomers resist change and excludes them from a brainstorming session on innovation. However, later discovers they had valuable insights from past transformations. | Actively seek out and consider opposing evidence or viewpoints. |
| **Anchoring Bias** | Relying heavily on the first piece of information encountered when making decisions. | Causes employees to rely on outdated generational expectations, hindering adaptability. | During salary negotiations, a Gen Z employee accepts a modest initial offer, unaware that others in the same role, particularly older employees, had negotiated much higher packages. | Avoid fixation on initial information by gathering a range of data points before making decisions – question assumptions |

| | | | | |
|---|---|---|---|---|
| **Availability Heuristic** | Overestimating the importance of information that comes to mind easily. | Amplifies visible generational conflicts, overshadowing collaborative successes. | A Gen X leader disproportionately assigns critical tasks to Millennials, recalling a recent instance where a Gen Z team member missed a deadline, even though it was an exception. | Base decisions on data and research, not just what comes to mind easily. |
| **Framing Effect** | Drawing different conclusions based on how information is presented. | Alters perceptions of generational inputs based on how feedback or ideas are presented. | A Baby Boomer executive introduces a hybrid work policy, framing it as a necessity for younger generations, unintentionally alienating older employees who see it as undervaluing their in-office contributions. | Reframe information in multiple ways to ensure decisions aren't overly influenced by presentation. |

| | | | | |
|---|---|---|---|---|
| **Hindsight Bias** | Believing an event was predictable after it has already happened. | Fuels blame in intergenerational disputes by assuming past events were predictable. | After a project failure, a Gen Z employee remarks, "It was obvious this approach wouldn't work," dismissing the collective team's decision-making process involving all generations. | Document decisions and their rationale to separate past predictions from outcomes. |
| **Overconfidence Bias** | Overestimating one's abilities, knowledge, or control over a situation. | Leads to dismissing younger or older colleagues' inputs due to overestimating one's expertise. | A Gen X supervisor insists on a familiar method for launching a product, ignoring the Gen Z team's data-driven pitch, only to see the approach underperform in a digital-first market. | Regularly validate your knowledge and predictions with evidence and feedback. |

| | | | | |
|---|---|---|---|---|
| **Negativity Bias** | Focusing more on negative experiences or information than positive ones. | Focuses on generational differences, overshadowing shared goals or achievements. | A Boomer manager focuses on the one negative feedback from a Gen Z team member in a 360° review, ignoring overwhelming positive input from others. | Balance negative feedback with positive perspectives to gain a well-rounded view. |
| **Status Quo Bias** | Preferring things to remain the same rather than change. | Resists adopting new practices or technologies introduced by younger generations. | A Millennial team lead resists adopting a new AI tool suggested by Gen Z employees, fearing disruption to the current workflow, even though it promises efficiency gains. | Question default choices and actively explore alternative options for improvement. |
| **Self-Serving Bias** | Attributing successes to oneself and failures to external factors. | Creates friction as individuals credit their generation for successes while blaming others for failures. | After a project's success, a Gen Z member credits their tech-savviness, but when it fails, blames the lack of vision from older generations. | Reflect on outcomes objectively, separating personal ego from external factors. |

| **Recency Bias** | The tendency to focus more on recent events or information while overlooking historical trends or data. | Can lead to overvaluing the latest trends or younger employees' recent performance, potentially alienating older generations with valuable long-term experience. | A Gen X recruiter heavily prioritizes Gen Z candidates for digital roles based on their recent performance in an innovation challenge, overlooking older candidates with relevant expertise. | Consider trends or patterns over a longer timeframe, not just recent events. |
|---|---|---|---|---|
| **Loss Aversion** | The inclination to prefer avoiding losses rather than acquiring equivalent gains. | May cause resistance to innovation or risk-taking, creating friction between generations with different attitudes toward change. | A Boomer employee resists retiring, fearing the perceived loss of their professional identity, even when presented with consulting opportunities that could utilize their expertise. | Frame decisions in terms of potential gains and long-term value, not immediate losses. |

| **Sunk Cost** | The tendency to continue investing in a decision due to past investments, even when it no longer makes sense. | Could result in maintaining outdated processes or technologies favored by older generations, frustrating younger employees eager for progress. | A Gen X manager continues investing in outdated software chosen years ago despite Gen Z's insistence on transitioning to a modern, cost-effective platform. | Focus on future benefits and costs rather than what's already invested. |
|---|---|---|---|---|

## Why Do We Have Inaccurate Beliefs about Age? (Stereotypes and Meta Stereotypes)

Emerging research in industrial-organizational psychology explores age-related beliefs from two interconnected perspectives. The first focuses on *age stereotypes,* which examine the content and effects of beliefs about individuals from specific age groups. The second, a newer concept known as *age meta-stereotypes*, delves into what we believe others think about us based on our age group. In an age-diverse workplace, these processes often occur simultaneously – employees may form quick judgments about others (stereotypes) while also assuming others are making judgments about them (meta-stereotypes). Let's delve deeper into these concepts and their implications.

A **Stereotype** is an oversimplified, fixed belief about a particular group of people, often based on generalized assumptions rather than individual experiences. In the context of a multi-generational workforce, stereotypes can include views like 'Baby Boomers are resistant to technology,' 'Gen X is workaholic,' 'Millennials are entitled, or 'Gen Z is too dependent on technology.' While these generalizations may contain an element of truth in certain contexts, they often fail to reflect the diversity of individual traits within a generation. Stereotypes can hinder collaboration by creating biases, fostering misunderstandings, and limiting opportunities for growth. I have listed some of the common stereotypes in the Generational Cheat Sheet section.

**Meta-stereotypes** are beliefs about how one's own group is stereotyped by others. For instance, Millennials may assume older colleagues perceive them as lazy, or Gen X might believe younger coworkers view them as inflexible. These meta-stereotypes can create defensive behaviors, amplify generational divides, and inhibit open communication.

**Meta-stereotypes** are beliefs about how one's own group is stereotyped by others. For instance, Millennials may assume older colleagues perceive them as lazy, or Gen X might believe younger coworkers view them as inflexible. These meta-stereotypes can create defensive behaviors, amplify generational divides, and inhibit open communication. To overcome stereotypes and meta-stereotypes, organizations can foster intergenerational dialogue, encourage mentorship programs that pair employees from different age groups and emphasize individual strengths over generational labels. Building awareness through unconscious bias training and creating inclusive environments where all generations feel valued is crucial to bridging these gaps. Some examples of meta-stereotypes:

**Gen Z Meta-Stereotype:**
*Belief: 'Older colleagues think we're glued to our phones and lack interpersonal skills.'*
*Overcome: Showcase strong communication by actively contributing to meetings and initiating in-person collaborations.*

**Millennial Meta-Stereotype:**
*Belief: 'Boomers think we're entitled and only care about quick promotions.'*
*Overcome: Demonstrate commitment by taking on challenging projects and seeking mentorship to show a growth mindset.*

**Gen X Meta-Stereotype:**
*Belief: 'Younger generations view us as outdated and resistant to change.'*
*Overcome: Engage in digital upskilling initiatives and openly support innovative ideas to challenge this perception.*

**Baby Boomer Meta-Stereotype:**
*Belief: 'Younger coworkers think we're too slow to adapt to technology.'*
*Overcome: Actively participate in tech training sessions and collaborate with younger colleagues on digital projects to share expertise.*

## How Do Inaccurate Beliefs about Age Affect Our Workplaces?

In a lab experiment, undergraduate students were tasked with training individuals on a computer task using Google's chat function. The trainees, also undergraduates, were asked to learn from the training and then perform the task. Researchers manipulated the perceived age of both the trainer and trainee using photos and voice-modifying software to make them appear either older (around 54 years) or younger (around 24 years).

Stereotypes about older individuals' ability to learn new tasks significantly impacted the training process. When trainers believed they were instructing an older person, they set lower expectations and delivered less effective training compared to when they thought they were teaching a younger individual. This highlights how age stereotypes can directly result in poorer training, which in turn may hinder learning and negatively affect job performance.

Moreover, beliefs about how others perceive one's age group – known as *meta-stereotypes* – can also disrupt workplace behavior. These beliefs can lead to negative responses, such as workplace conflicts or avoidance behaviors, like withdrawing from interactions with colleagues. The combined effects of stereotypes and meta-stereotypes pose significant challenges to fostering effective workplace dynamics.

## How to De-Bias Our Biases and Overcome Stereotypes?

In 2019, I delivered my first Ted Talk which is titled 'Thinking Straight Is Hard – Escaping the Mind Traps.' This was a talk on behavioral biases. I covered some of the biases to help audiences see how they hinders our decision-making. In the end, I gave a simple three-point call to action on how to overcome biases. I believe these three points are so very crucial and relevant, and I recommend them below as a way to overcome biases.

### Creating Greater Self-Awareness:

Self-awareness helps individuals recognize their own biases and stereotypes, fostering an understanding of how these beliefs influence their interactions. For instance, a manager who assumes Gen Z employees prefer remote work might learn through reflection that this assumption isn't universally true. By becoming aware of their biases, individuals can challenge preconceived notions and make more objective decisions. Self-awareness also promotes empathy, allowing people to see beyond generational labels and value individual contributions. Companies spend millions in helping leaders become more self-aware, especially when you start managing people or teams. The greater the awareness you have, the better your chance of succeeding. One common way to do this is to administer a self-awareness instrument. An instrument is a questionnaire which seeks your preferred way of doing things and gives you a report indicating your predominant preference. It could be a personality tool like MBTI, FIRO-B, or 360 Instrument, where multiple stakeholders rate you on different parameters. These stakeholders are bosses, peers, direct reports, customers, vendors, regulators and others. The more we can have people share their views, the greater the data to help us become more self-aware. Many companies will also have leaders go through an instrument when they get promoted to a new role, indicating their strengths and potential challenges. In addition to the instrument, you can do the following simple steps to improve your self-awareness. Here are some additional ways to increase self-awareness:

- **Reflect on Personal Assumptions:** Regularly question your beliefs about different generations. Ask yourself, '*Is this assumption based on facts or stereotypes*?' Recognizing these biases is the first step toward breaking them.
- **Seek Feedback:** Invite colleagues from various generations to share how your actions or decisions impact

them. Honest feedback provides insight into unconscious behaviors that may perpetuate biases.

- **Engage in Active Listening:** Focus on understanding others' perspectives without judgment during conversations. Listening helps uncover the individuality behind generational labels.
- **Participate in Diversity Training:** Attend workshops or programs that raise awareness about generational differences and offer strategies for bridging gaps.
- **Practice Empathy:** Put yourself in the shoes of colleagues from other generations. Understand their challenges, values, and motivations to appreciate their unique perspectives.
- **Monitor Reactions and Behaviors:** Notice how you react to others' ideas or work styles. Journaling these moments can help identify triggers and patterns linked to biases.
- **Cultivate Curiosity:** Instead of assuming, ask questions about how different generations approach work, communication, and problem-solving. This fosters deeper understanding and respect.

## Using Decision Diaries:

A decision diary involves recording the thought process, assumptions, and outcomes behind key decisions. This practice helps individuals identify patterns of bias and assess whether stereotypes influence their choices. For example, if a team lead consistently excludes Baby Boomers from tech-related projects, reviewing the diary can reveal this pattern and prompt corrective action. Additionally, the diary fosters accountability, encouraging more deliberate, fair, and inclusive decision-making.

In the earlier story of the large financial services company and its senior leadership, we also noticed that the team preferred hiring people who were similar to theirs. We administered a decision-making instrument. The instrument could be on personality, behaviors, strengths, etc. In this, it was decision making which had structured/unstructured on one axis and individual/together on the other. This means you can make decisions with either structured data or unstructured data. And in the second axis it is either done by yourself or with others. What we found is that 24 out of the 25 had a similar way of making decisions, which is always wanting structured information and preferred taking them individually. In a business environment, when information is not always available, and we have to make decisions as a group, this is a competency the team did not have. This bias was also seen when they were hiring new members. They preferred hiring people who were just like them.

Using Decision Diary, we asked them to track their key decisions over the next 8-10 months. The team had to write about the key problem and their desired and actual outcomes. In tracking these decisions, they realized many of the same biases came into play as they took key decisions. Seeing the decision diary for about a year helped them to see their pattern and thus overcome their biases.

## Activate System 2 Thinking

Activating System 2 Thinking requires creating intentional pauses to reflect before making judgments or decisions. Techniques like asking open-ended questions, gathering diverse viewpoints, and relying on data instead of assumptions can slow down impulsive reactions. Practices such as journaling thoughts, seeking feedback, and challenging the 'why' behind initial beliefs also engage analytical reasoning. For instance, when evaluating a colleague's work style, focus on their actual performance metrics rather than stereotypes. These deliberate efforts encourage a more thoughtful, objective approach, reducing the influence of biases. By practicing System 2 Thinking, workplaces can foster fairer, more inclusive interactions that value individual strengths over generational labels.

Understanding biases, stereotypes, and meta-stereotypes is essential to bridging a multi-generational workforce because it uncovers hidden assumptions that hinder collaboration and trust. By recognizing these influences, teams can break down barriers, appreciate individual strengths, and foster a culture of inclusion. This awareness not only enhances communication but also drives innovation and productivity, turning generational diversity into a strategic advantage.

## Personal Reflection Sheet

What are some of the Biases, Stereotypes, and Meta-Stereotypes you are seeing among different generations in your organization?

What steps are you taking to overcome the Biases and Stereotypes?

Please share your answer sheets and responses to www.learnwisely.in

CHAPTER 6

# Beyond the Surface: Learning the Context Behind the Perspectives

'Seek first to understand, then to be understood.'

— Stephen R. Covey

## Content Is King, but Context Is the Kingdom

After about a decade of consulting on leadership development work for firms across Asia, I've noticed that the problems companies want help with seem similar. We hear a range of issues: How can you help our high-potential middle managers become ready for senior positions (Strategic Thinkers)? How do we engage our young talent? How do we make our leaders more empathetic and reflective? How do they become better at influencing external stakeholders? How can leaders become good with feedback, difficult conversations, team collaboration, and so forth? So, which company operating today doesn't face these kinds of people challenges? Therefore, yes, the challenges are similar, but the context is NOT. What works as a solution in one firm will not work in another. What works for a firm in one industry may not work for another firm in the same industry. For example, feedback routines in a public sector firm (which could be very hierarchical) are markedly different from a start-up (with a flat structure). Culture in family-owned firms can be very fluid, largely influenced by promoters, versus a culture of large multinationals which could be much more structured and well-defined. Team collaboration will have a different design for each firm. Some will prefer stories, others will want outdoor activities, and many others will want simulations. Leadership development for many is a strong lever of who they are, and for many others, programs are done more as a necessity (if they are in a growth cycle and cannot afford high-end premium programs). So, each company's story is unique.

Drawing parallels, we know that every firm today has a minimum of three, possibly four, generations at work. We've looked at some of the **Points of Differences (PODs)** in the first section of the book - communication, values, ageism, and so on. Now, in the second half of the book, we will try to understand how to bridge the PODs through **Points of Parity (POPs)**. Perhaps the most important place for us to start is to understand each generation's context. As we will see, the context becomes the foundation of their beliefs, which, in turn, becomes the behavior they bring to work. In this chapter, we will explore multiple generations, examining their global and Indian contexts to understand how key events have shaped their identities, values, and perspectives.

## My Generational Context

My parents were born in the early 1940s, just shortly before India gained independence from British rule. According to the Western definition of generation experts, they were a part of the 'Baby Boomer' generation. We will understand the various definitions of different generations shortly. I was born in the early 1970s; therefore, I am part of 'Generation X'. My son and nephew are Gen Zer's (born in 2003 and 2005 respectively). My grandfather passed away before I was born, but I have memories of my grandmother till about my early 30s. The most common kinds of literature that document generation are largely in the American context. For me, it is the childhood experience of growing up in India. There were many times I would recall my father saying, 'Your generation cannot work hard the way we did,' and I say the same to my son, 'You just don't know what hard work is.'

Today, as I look back, I agree with my father's statement. Yet the context in which my father came from was different than the one given to me, and the same goes for my son. My father was the first generation that grew up in the post-Independence era (1950-60s), and there was a high degree of nationalistic spirit in his generation; hearing tales of freedom fighters like Gandhi and other leaders carried forward to his generation from his parents. The country was rebuilding itself, and, in many ways, a new journey for Independent India was unfolding. India had adopted a socialistic approach to running an economy and was reaching out to post-war allies which shaped the way the country saw the role of government and industries. They had to do well for the taste of a better life. In this context, I saw my father working hard professionally to ensure his children had a virtuous life. He travelled extensively across the globe for work, and on each of these trips, the money he would save from consultation work was hard-earned for the family.

We got a TV in our house when I was in about grade 5 and a car around grade 7. I witnessed the quintessential effort of the first generation to sow the seeds of hard work to build a better life for the next generation. I grew up just before the liberalization wave of the Indian economy (the 1980s and early 90s) by which time things had dramatically changed. India had the Indian Institute of Technology (IITs) and the Indian Institute of Management (IIMs) well established. More businesses were entering the country, and we were becoming a consumer-led society.

When I completed middle school, I had a chance to go to the US and stay there for many years. With a good education in the US and then doing reasonably well professionally, we were the typical middle-class family who continued to aspire for a better life from the foundation my father had built. By better life, I mean a good house, travels abroad, cars and giving our children a good education. And, of course, my son saw a totally different India in the early 2000s, when it grew to be a very different country in a spell of 75 years. He has travelled abroad a few times during his teenage years, sees all the global brands in India and has access to the best educational resources. For him, all of this seems to be a given.

He finds it hard to relate that TV could only have two channels in the late 1970s and early 80s. Radio was a common medium of entertainment for the family. Visiting family during festivals was something everyone enjoyed and looked forward to, and not simply communicating through FaceTime, WhatsApp or other social media platforms. In those days, seeing a global brand in India was a big deal. I recall distinct memories in which you had to pre-book or request a 'trunk call' if you wished to dial internationally. The waiting period to get a Bajaj scooter was 10 years. Flying was an adventure experience for the rich and wealthy – all memories of the 80s.

Each of these events was a precursor to the prevailing context in which the earlier generation operated and shaped their values and beliefs. My father's focus was completely on establishing himself financially so the next generation wouldn't go through the same hardships that he did. For my son, he is growing up in a world of plenty. So, for me, the worry is of a different kind. I worry for him and his generation to appreciate the value of money instead of taking it for granted. He is growing up where everything comes on a platter, and he can get everything with a click of a button. We will explore what this shift of context means for the preceding generations and generations that follow. But before we thumb through further, we need to understand the relevance of understanding generations better.

## What Is a Generation?

Karl Mannheim, the influential German sociologist, defined a generation as a group of individuals of similar ages whose members have experienced a noteworthy historical event within a set period of time. A key point, he emphasized, is that a major historical event has to occur and involve the individuals at a young age, thus shaping their lives, as later experiences will tend to receive meaning from those early experiences.

Mannheim stresses that not every generation will develop an original and distinctive consciousness. Whether a generation succeeds in developing a distinctive consciousness significantly depends on the pace of social change. Social change can occur gradually, without the need for major historical events, but those events are more likely to occur in times of accelerated social and cultural change. Additionally, members of a generation are internally stratified by their location, culture, class, etc.; thus, they may view different events from different angles and may not be totally homogenous. So, those of us who grew up in the same country also had unique teen experiences based on our family's socio-economic background, our parents' philosophies, and a host of other factors. But the prominent events shared particularly during formative teen years give your generation its defining characteristics.

In short, we can't predict when one generation will end and another will begin or what will be enough of a change to push us from one generation to another. Similar to a recession, you don't know it has happened until you are in the middle of it and can't predict when it will end. However, you know and feel that something is different.

Let us now understand how generation experts have classified the various generations and what shaped them for who they were. We will look at the events both in the Western context (European and US) and in the Indian context. For the Indian context, we have explained generations after the Second World War or after Independent India.

## The Greatest Generation: Born Between 1902 to 1927

The Greatest Generation, also known as the G.I Generation, is the demographic cohort following the Lost Generation and preceding the Silent Generation. This generation is generally defined as people born from 1902 to 1927. They were shaped by the Great Depression and were the primary participants in World War II.

## The Silent Generation: Born Between 1928 to 1945

The Silent Generation began in 1928 because there was an enormous boom of babies after World War II. The Silent Generation ended in 1945 because World War II ended in the same year, and the birth rates that characterized the Silent Generation came to a swift end.

The Silent Generation were children of the Great Depression whose parents, having revelled in the highs of the roaring twenties, now faced great economic hardship and struggled to provide even the basic necessities to their families. Before reaching their teens, they shared with their parents the horrors of World War II but through children's eyes. Many lost their fathers or older siblings who were killed in the war. They saw the fall of Nazism and the catastrophic devastation capable of the nuclear bomb. When the Silent Generation began coming of age after World War II, they were faced with a devastating social order within which they would spend their early adulthood. They were an eyewitness to a new enemy in Communism via the betrayal of post-war agreements and the rise of the Soviet Union.

Unlike the previous generation who had fought for 'changing the system', the Silent Generation was about 'working within the system.' They did this by keeping their heads down and working hard, thus earning themselves the 'silent' label. Their attitudes leaned toward not being risk-takers and playing it safe. From their childhood experiences during the Depression and the insistence from their parents to be frugal, they tended to be thrifty and even miserly. They preferred to maximize the property's lifespan, i.e., 'get their money's worth.' This led to hoarding in the guise of 'not being wasteful.'

## The Baby Boomer Generation: Born Between 1946 to 1964

The Baby Boomers are people born during the post-World War II 'Baby Boom' roughly during the years 1946 to 1964. In the years following World War II, most Western nations experienced a spike in births as they slowly recovered from the economic hardships experienced during wartime. This group was quite diverse and experienced many social changes early on; in fact, older generations noticed a generation gap early in the Baby Boomer generation because it was the second post-war generation to emerge. Perhaps this generation gap was noticed more than during the Silent Generation's post-war culture boom because the economy and technology progressed even further.

This new generation of Baby Boomers experienced unprecedented economic growth and prosperity throughout their lifetime. They entered the world in a time of relative hardship, but thanks to education, government subsidies, rising property prices and technological advancements, they emerged as a successful and affluent generation.

**The Indian Context:** In India, the 1940s and 1950s saw the birth of India as an independent nation. Teens witnessed Mahatma Gandhi's non-violent, civil disobedient campaign for independence, the end of the British Raj, and Gandhi's assassination. It was a time of patriotic pride, with the resurgence of Indian traditions and the establishment of a democratic republic with elections. But the living conditions in India, at the time, were difficult because of a poor economy, short life expectancies, low rates of literacy, mass impoverishment, stalled industrial development, and destitute farmers. The India-Pakistan partition of 1947 also marked the beginning of a long border conflict.

For individuals in this generation in India, patriotic pride over the newly established independent nation blended with loyalty to family and community success was defined as obedience to traditional practices while finding ways to participate in this new India.

## Generation X: Born Between 1965 to 1979

Generation X came after the Baby Boomers generation and typically covers people born between the mid-1960s and the early 1980s. Gen X was shaped by global political events that occurred during this generation's youth phase. Generation X also overlaps with another group called Sandwich Generation. This modern generation has gotten its place in this slot to characterize middle-aged individuals who, due to increased life expectancy and later parenthood, simultaneously support both aging parents and growing children.

The Indian Context: India, during these same years, shifted to a socialist economic model under Indira Gandhi's leadership: nationalization of industries, public works, social reforms, and public investment in education. Events such as the nationalization of 14 banks, close to insolvency, the introduction of Rajdhani Express, and the setup of the Indian Space Research Organization (ISRO) helped shape this generation's culture and upbringing. Political factions grew, and the Indian National Congress split into two: Old and New Congress. India signed a 20-year treaty of friendship with the Soviet Union; its first break from non-alignment. Wars around borders continued: Sino-Indian War, Indo-Pakistan War of 1965, and the Indo-Pakistan War of 1971 (Independence of Bangladesh). The rupee was liberalized and underwent severe devaluation. The 'Green Revolution' improved agricultural productivity, enabling India to feed its population self-sufficiently after two decades of food imports. Towards the end of the period, during the Indian Emergency of 1975-77, Indira Gandhi was accused of corruption, ruled by decree, suspended elections and civil liberties, and was removed from power by the opposition.

For teens in India at this time, economic options were limited due to the sluggish economy; personal options were heavily influenced by the family, group, or caste into which one was born. These constraints were giving way to the power of education, which was increasingly available for the best and brightest. For those who were able and successful their focus was on getting out of India to obtain higher education and work in the UK or US. There was a growing diaspora who not only took care of and retained close ties with those in India but began to make investments in the country's economic future. As compared to previous generations, Gen X was more open to diversity and learned to embrace differences such as religion, sexual orientation, class, race and ethnicity. Similar to US teens' experience with Watergate, the Indian Emergency left this generation with skepticism of political leaders.

## Generation Y: Born Between 1980 to 1995

Following Generation X, Generation Y covers the generations born between the 1980s and 1995. These individuals are sometimes referred to as Gen Y or the Millennial Generation. Generation Y has been molded by the technological revolution that occurred throughout their life. Gen Y grew up with technology, so being connected and tech-savvy is part of their genes. Equipped with the latest technology and gadgets, such as phones, laptops and tablets, Gen Y is online and, in the network, 24/7, 365 days a year. Many Millennials grew up seeing their Baby Boomer parents working all day and night doing stressful jobs, shaping their views about the workforce and the need for work-life balance.

**The Indian Context:** Teens saw Indira Gandhi assassinated by her two bodyguards and succeeded by her son Rajiv Gandhi, who instituted a number of important reforms: loosened business regulations, lowered restrictions on foreign investment imports, and reduced bureaucracy. Rajiv Gandhi also led the country in a major expansion of the telecommunications industry, space programs, software industry and information technology sector. Political conflict continued, and

Rajiv Gandhi's image as an honest politician was shattered by the Bofors scandal, and he was later killed by a suicide bomber. P.V. Narasimha Rao became the next Prime Minister and initiated further economic liberalization and reform. Still, over 75% of 1980s IIT graduates emigrated to the US.

Gen Ys in India shared the generation's global sense of immediacy, coupled with the excitement of being part of the country's first wave of broad economic opportunity. As a result, young employees in India tend to share the rapid tempo of US Gen Y's ambitions, but with a greater emphasis on financial reward as the desired outcome. They have come of age in an exciting, dynamic country with significant economic opportunity. Most are entrepreneurial, business savvy, technologically capable, and connected. Their mental model is heavily influenced by India's rich, complex democracy. They easily accept diversity of opinion as well as the Western heritage of laws and customs left from the old days of British rule, making them strongly suited for global interaction.

The late 1990s and 2000s also saw the development of a large part of the middle-class population and increased the demand for the production of many consumer goods in many ways – a situation reminiscent of the US. The Indian economy grew under liberalization and reform policies; the country was stable and prosperous, and political power changed hands without incident. India became a prestigious educational powerhouse and a respected source of IT talent. By

2008, 34 Indian companies were listed in the Forbes Global 2000 ranking.

## Generation Z: Born Between 1996 to 2012

Born between 1996 and 2012, falling between the ages of 8 and 29, Gen Z is coming of age in a time of global unrest, divisive politics and the ubiquitous presence of technology. Many label them as Millennials 2.0, but that could not be further from the truth. Gen Z has grown up in a time with active shooter drills in their schools. They have seen visible impacts of climate change, 'fake news' and '#Me-too' as trending topics. They are a generation determined to be highly connected with living in an era of high-tech communication, technology-driven lifestyles and prolific use of social media.

## The Technology-Aware Generation

Gen Z has had a unique relationship with a powerful force of modern technology since birth. Unlike Millennials, who witnessed the introduction and rise of social media, tablets, smartphones and the mobility that allows them to access it all in an instant, Gen Z was born into it. They are true digital natives, the first to grow up online, connected to vast amounts of timely, global information and instantly socially connected to friends, businesses, other organizations and even celebrities. They have never known a world where they couldn't instantly connect and look up the answer to any question that crossed their mind. There is no need to ask anyone or to hide from the unknown. They can figure it out for themselves in their preferred domain: online. With so much of Gen Z's social life centred around the digital domain, significant percentages prefer socializing online than in real life. More than half say it's easier to chat digitally or more convenient.

Gen Zs are highly informed and want to take charge of their lives and their futures. With the unique social and familial setting, they are a more self-aware, self-reliant and driven generation than the previous one. So, it is not surprising that they are less loyal to companies who don't often support their cause and value system. They believe in standing up for global issues, whether it is gender equality, environment, poverty and hunger, health and disease, education, ethics, and governance. They are also intuitive, innovative, uber-productive, goal-oriented and realistic. So, they are entrepreneurial.

### Generation Alpha: Born between (2010 and 2024)

The first fully digital-native generation, growing up with AI, voice assistants, and immersive tech: They experience personalized learning tools and are influenced by diverse, inclusive societal values. Sustainability and mental health are integral to their lives.

**The Indian Context:** This cohort is witnessing the expansion of India's digital revolution, embracing online education, OTT platforms, and evolving urban lifestyles. Rooted in family values, they also face unique challenges like balancing traditional norms with modern aspirations.

### Generation Beta: Born (2025-2039)

Expected to inherit advancements in AI, quantum computing, and biotechnology. They'll navigate the challenges of over-automation and climate change while likely being global citizens from an early age, shaped by rapid technological and cultural convergence.

**The Indian Context:** Projected to grow up in an even more tech-saturated environment, they'll be critical players in India's push for innovation. They are likely to engage deeply in global issues like sustainability while navigating the juxtaposition of local traditions and hyper-modern influences.

**Generational Context:** Exploring my family's stories highlights the diverse experiences we have encountered in both childhood and adulthood. Each of these experiences has shaped distinct cultural influences within our respective generations. Today, as I reflect while writing this book, I believe Generational Progression serves as a reminder that each generation sees progression that previous ones have never seen. I believe that we are better because we each have experiences that shape our identities. It means we can learn from each other's experiences and understand that our generations are so different.

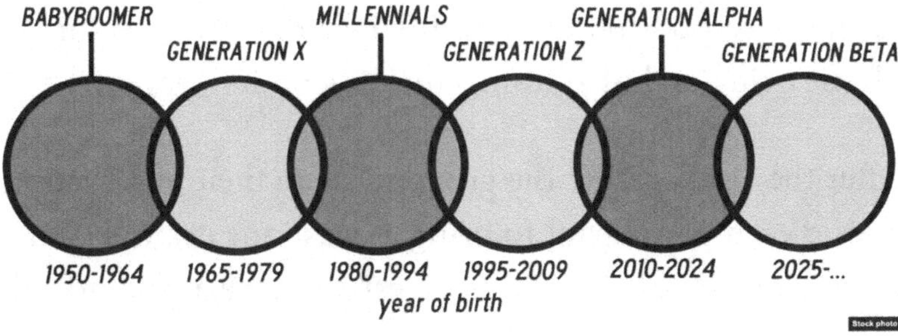


Fig 6.0 Understanding the Generational Timelines (@voanews.com)

## Overcoming Generational Beliefs and Assumptions (Three Activities)

We've seen in Chapter 5 the various stereotypes, meta-stereotypes and key biases we carry about each generation and ways to overcome them. In this chapter, we go beneath the iceberg and understand the context that has shaped their thinking and values. To further extrapolate, how do we build more Points of Parity caused by generational assumptions? I recommend three specific activities you can try in your organization to unleash generational power and harmony.

### I. Belief Check-In (Audit)

Encourage employees to spend a week actively observing age-based assumptions in the workplace, paying attention to their actions and those of others. For example, they might notice a team leader dismissing a younger employee's request for more responsibility as 'entitled' or observe a senior employee being excluded from a meeting on innovation.

After the week, gather the group to share their observations, asking each participant to bring at least one example. These discussions may be sensitive, so establish clear ground rules to maintain a constructive tone. Encourage participants to describe what they observed without assigning intent. For instance, 'Input from younger teammates is dismissed quickly,' instead of 'Senior leaders dismiss younger teammates because they undervalue their input.' Foster openness to feedback and prompt the group to reflect on how age-based assumptions – whether rooted in truth or not – affect team dynamics, engagement, and performance.

Schedule a follow-up session a few weeks later to revisit the topic, ensure accountability, and incorporate awareness into daily practices.

### Shift Your Perspective

Recognizing stereotypes is a crucial first step, but addressing them requires active effort. Generational assumptions often lead to misattributing differences or projecting negative intent. Shifting perspectives involves reassessing whether these beliefs align with reality or reflect personal biases. Encourage employees to explore why colleagues from different generations might behave differently and to approach those behaviors with curiosity rather than judgment.

### II. Observe – Analyze – Act

This exercise broadens understanding among team members of different generations.

1. **Observe:** Identify a specific frustration with someone from a different generation.
2. **Analyze:** Reflect on your initial interpretation of their behavior.
3. **Act:** Reevaluate your assumption and consider alternative explanations. Employees can also seek group input for new perspectives.

### Take Advantage of Differences

After addressing assumptions and reframing perspectives, focus on leveraging generational differences as strengths. Collaborate to benefit from one another's unique experiences, insights, and networks.

Psychological safety is essential for fostering this collaboration. Research by Harvard's Amy Edmondson highlights its importance in creating an environment where employees feel secure sharing new ideas and differing viewpoints. However, perceived generational competition – often amplified by sensational media – can erode trust. Rebuilding trust begins with creating spaces, such as roundtable discussions, where diverse perspectives are acknowledged and valued.

By cultivating psychological safety and embracing productive differences, teams can harness the full potential of their age-diverse workforce.

## III. Generational Dialogue Circle

Leaders of intergenerational teams should establish monthly meetings to foster collaboration and improve team dynamics. This process unfolds in two key stages:

### 1. Finding Common Ground

While leveraging differences is essential, team members must first recognize their shared purpose to function effectively. Research shows that aligning on common goals is critical for team performance. Intergenerational teams often find it challenging to establish this shared foundation. During the first dialogue session, prompt team members to answer questions like:

- Why does this team exist?
- What shared goals do we aim to accomplish?

These discussions help teammates see themselves as collaborators working toward a joint mission, fostering psychological safety and a sense of unity.

### 2. Encouraging Fresh Insights

In subsequent sessions, guide discussions with questions designed to surface new ideas and perspectives:

- What are we, as a team, doing well to achieve our shared goals?
- What actions or behaviors are hindering our progress?
- What untapped opportunities should we explore?
- If you were in charge, what would you start, stop, or continue doing?

The aim is not to force immediate resolutions but to uncover fresh perspectives and amplify voices that may have previously gone unheard. Differences of opinion– and even conflict – may arise, which is natural. Redirect conversations to the team's shared goals, emphasizing that differing viewpoints enrich collaboration and drive success.

The aim is not to force immediate resolutions but to uncover fresh perspectives and amplify voices that may have previously gone unheard. Differences of opinion– and even conflict – may arise, which is natural. Redirect conversations to the team's shared goals, emphasizing that differing viewpoints enrich collaboration and drive success.

## Promoting Mutual Learning

To maximize the potential of intergenerational teams, members must believe in the value of learning from colleagues of all age groups. The ultimate objective is a culture of mutual learning, where teaching and learning occur in a continuous, reciprocal loop.

## Mutual Mentoring

To nurture this environment, organizations and managers can implement two-way 'mutual mentoring' programs. Research shows such initiatives enhance skill development, individual engagement, and collective motivation.

## Building a Mentorship Culture

1. Establish an Informal Network: Start by asking team members what they want to learn and what they can teach. Since potential mentors may be modest about their expertise, offer suggestions based on observed strengths.
2. Identify Natural Pairings: Match individuals based on complementary skills and interests, such as pairing someone adept at creating TikTok videos with a colleague eager to learn or connecting seasoned professionals with those looking to expand their networks. While not every pairing needs to be cross-generational, ensure all age groups participate as both learners and instructors.
3. Kick-off and Sustain the Network: Host an initial meeting where a few mentors briefly showcase their exper-

tise. Encourage participants to reach out to mentors who align with their interests. To maintain momentum, send monthly reminders to keep the conversations active.

Generational stereotypes like 'OK Boomer,' 'Gen X Cynics,' 'Entitled Millennials,' and 'Gen Z Snowflakes' have entrenched us in divisive name-calling. At the same time, efforts to downplay differences can overlook the unique strengths age diversity brings to the table. Especially in a time of rapid workplace transformation, leaders must view intergenerational teams as opportunities to enrich diversity, equity, and inclusion (DEI) efforts rather than challenges to navigate.

While mistrust between older and younger workers can create a culture of competition and resentment, well-managed age-diverse teams unlock a powerful exchange of skills, knowledge, and networks, benefiting individuals and organizations alike.

CHAPTER 7

# When Careers Collide: Managing Spillover in a Diverse Workforce

> 'When careers collide, the challenge isn't just balancing priorities but harmonizing purpose. Managing spillover requires clarity, empathy, and the courage to redefine boundaries.'
>
> —Satya Nadella, CEO of Microsoft

## Client Story

For many years, we worked with a large conglomerate in manufacturing and conducted a senior leadership program at their group academy. Our program had participants from across the group, and we used to meet leaders from many parts of the business (manufacturing and services). The theme of the program focused on understanding outside trends, building an inclusive team, managing stakeholders and creating your legacy.

In one of the editions, we heard a story about a senior leader who was a successful CFO in the group business and had held that position for more than 15 years. He was very good at what he did and had created a good brand in the organization. However, he consciously opted to be in that position for many years despite opportunities for new roles. The younger colleagues in the finance function felt they could not rise the ladder as this leader just wasn't going or retiring. Many quit and went to another role within the group; others quit altogether.

However, two years after hearing the story, group HR and business leaders ensured that whether this leader liked it or not, he had to create room for his younger direct reports and find something different for himself.

This dilemma is increasingly becoming common in companies and economies, where many workers remain in the workforce past retirement age or stay in the same role for extended periods, limiting opportunities for younger employees who either endure years of frustration or choose to quit. These constraints hold back high-potential younger workers as old ones stay around and create boom and bust cycles of talent demand. This problem can create an intergenerational conflict which is often called 'Career Spillovers.'

Internal and external forces cause such spillovers. Internally, these spillovers can occur when the company is limited in its ability to provide opportunities for its employees to move up, so one's advancement comes at the cost of coworkers. This means that when older workers delay retirement or stay long in one role (because they have become so good at it) younger workers' careers stall.

Externally, forces such as industry conditions and macro-economic trends can also shape a person's career growth ladder. When sales orders aren't coming in, and the client base isn't increasing, the business can't grow. If the business isn't growing, it cannot create more opportunities to move up. Since startups or young firms grow more quickly than more established firms, the spillover effect is felt in large firms. The slow-growing companies lose good talent to fast-growing firms making it harder for them to grow for new growth.

Today, many companies across the globe are increasing their retirement age due to pressures from competition and also how the talent demographics play out in their market. Older employees in such situations tend to benefit if they are in high positions because there is generally less turnover during the last few years of their careers. However, external factors like growth alone don't play a role; often, a firm's inability to create 'career capacity' can affect itself and its employees. There is increasing evidence that neglecting career opportunities or being unable to provide them can lead to attrition, especially among high-potential employees. Firms that realize this and work towards a strategic talent management approach also have to deal with older workers staying longer as younger workers want them to move on. So, what are some ways to address this intergenerational conflict of talent?

## Promote Leadership Renewal – Championing Fresh Perspectives

If companies can limit the amount of time senior employees can stay in their position, advancement is designed into the firm. Mandatory retirement policies or role changes encourage turnover at the top. This is good for those aspiring for senior roles, but more importantly, it benefits the leader. Leaders often fall into what is called **Competency Traps.** A Competency Trap is all about becoming good at something to the extent that you start liking what you do and just want to do more of it. You settle into what becomes either a comfort zone or, at times, a plateau. This limits the leader's own potential to unleash other competencies. Often, when we've become good in a role, our thinking and networks are also filtered by the people we see and work with. This can often create blind spots and can especially limit leaders to building an 'Enterprise-Wide View.' I have seen this in many high-potential programs where a functional leader is aspiring for a senior leader's role but is not willing to give up skills of their domain feeling insecure about what would happen if the next role or assignment fails. By being in one more role where there is no limit, they are blocking their growth but also limiting upward movement.

A Competency Trap is all about becoming good at something to the extent that you start liking what you do and just want to do more of it. You settle into what becomes either a comfort zone or, at times, a plateau. This limits the leader's own potential to unleash other competencies. Often, when we've become good in a role, our thinking and networks are also filtered by the people we see and work with. This can often create blind spots and can especially limit leaders to building an 'Enterprise-Wide View.'

The one drawback of a fixed-tenured rule is that it can also force valuable talent out of the firm. Also, decreased job security through mandatory terms may also make the job less desirable. While younger workers want older workers to get out of the way, they probably don't want the same rule applied to their own situation.

Involuntary departures can be hard but can be made less painful if firms facilitate post-departure careers. For example, Home Depot recruits and hires thousands of retired construction workers making most of their expertise on the sales floor. The National Institute of Health in the US, whose workforce is over 50, actively recruits at 50-plus job fairs and offers benefits such as flexible schedules, remote work and exercises. This practice is also common in public sector banks where retired executives, either as general or senior managers, come back in the capacity of consultants or faculty in learning functions to share their knowledge and experience over the years. Michelin rehires retirees to oversee projects, foster community relations, and facilitate employee mentoring. These practices help leaders overcome insecurity about relinquishing their roles while also allowing them to contribute meaningfully and enable younger talent to grow simultaneously.

## Widening Leadership Pipeline

One way to circumvent the mandatory retirement path could be to add more positions. Expanding to create career capacity creates more positions without losing what's there.

**The benefits of doing this could be:**

Diverse Perspectives: More leadership positions can bring a wider range of expertise, enabling better-informed decisions and innovative solutions. For instance, companies with separate Chief Data, Digital, and Technology Officers gain specialized insights that drive digital transformation from multiple angles.

**Strategic Focus:** Increasing leadership roles can support focusing on specialized areas critical to the company's strategy, such as sustainability or digital innovation. An example is the rise of Chief Sustainability Officers (CSOs) in companies prioritizing environmental impact, allowing these organizations to pursue green initiatives more effectively.

**Increased Mentorship and Development:** More senior roles can offer greater opportunities for mentorship and succession planning. Junior managers can benefit from having multiple leaders to learn from, enhancing the company's leadership pipeline. Google's layered leadership structure, with roles like VPs of engineering and product in addition to traditional C-suite, helps drive mentorship.

**Workload Distribution:** With more executives, responsibilities can be more evenly spread, reducing burnout and enabling each leader to focus on their function. This can lead to better organizational health and longevity of leaders in high-pressure roles.

**Improved Stakeholder Relationships:** A broader leadership team allows for more specialized roles in stakeholder management, such as Chief Customer Officers (CCOs) focusing solely on customer satisfaction and engagement. This enhances relationships with key stakeholders, ensuring a more customer-centric approach. However, this can create a top-heavy or often middle-heavy layer in the organization. I've seen a thin middle layer and a large line-level organization in many organizations with more VPs and SVPs. In World War II, there were 30 navy ships for every admiral. In addition to being expensive, it seemed there were more cooks in the kitchen which could often lead to slow and worse decisions. Everyone is in charge, so no one is in charge. One way to create more positions and avoid chaos would be to have a rotation policy so leaders or workers can take turns being in leadership positions. For instance, the Chinese telecom giant Huawei employs a unique leadership structure, with three deputy chairmen rotating as acting CEOs, each serving a six-month tenure.

Some of the disadvantages of this also include:

**Potential for Redundancy:** When roles overlap or functions aren't clearly defined, decision-making can become redundant and bureaucratic, delaying progress. For instance, organizations with a Chief Digital Officer (CDO) and a Chief Information Officer (CIO) may find it challenging to clearly delineate responsibilities, leading to confusion.

**Increased Operational Costs:** More leaders mean higher salaries and benefits expenses, which can strain the budget. This is especially true in industries with tight profit margins, where the ROI of additional senior roles can be harder to justify.

**Complex Decision-Making:** Having many voices at the top can slow decision-making, especially if there's a lack of alignment on strategic goals. For example, companies with a Chief Marketing Officer (CMO) and a Chief Brand Officer may face challenges in brand strategy if roles aren't clearly differentiated.

**Difficulty in Accountability:** With more positions, it can become harder to pinpoint accountability, as multiple leaders may have overlapping responsibilities. For instance, if both a Chief Product Officer and a Chief Innovation Officer are tasked with new product development, accountability for delays or issues may be blurred.

**Potential for Internal Competition:** When there are many leadership roles, competition for influence and resources can lead to internal politics. A classic example is the rivalry between Chief Operating Officers and Chief Financial Officers in companies where resource allocation is tightly controlled, potentially impacting overall performance.

## What's the Antidote?

So, a balanced approach to managing multiple top positions involves strategic clarity, role alignment, and streamlined processes.

## Define Clear Roles and Responsibilities

**1. Role Clarity:** Ensure that each leadership role has distinct, non-overlapping responsibilities. A well-defined charter for each role prevents ambiguity and duplication of effort and ensures each leader can focus on their unique contribution. Example: Companies like Google and Microsoft often publish role charters that outline specific responsibilities for positions like Chief Data Officer and Chief Information Officer, clearly differentiating their strategic focuses (e.g., data governance versus digital infrastructure).

**2. Establish Cross-Functional Collaboration Frameworks**

- **Regular Alignment Meetings:** Set up routine cross-functional meetings to align on strategy, shared objectives, and project updates. This helps leaders with intersecting roles, such as Chief Digital Officer and Chief Marketing Officer, coordinate effectively.
- **Task Forces and Steering Committees:** For strategic initiatives, form temporary teams composed of leaders from different functions to encourage collaboration rather than competition.

**Example:** Many organizations use a 'matrixed' approach for cross-functional projects, where leaders like the Chief Operations Officer and Chief Technology Officer are part of a steering committee for operational efficiency projects. Google, for example, has committees for cross-functional projects where they appoint a chairperson, a finance rep, a legal advisor, an HR rep, and a project lead. Many other firms like Boeing, Unilever, P&G have similar models.

### 3. Create Decision-Making Protocols

- **Clear Decision Rights:** Specify which roles have decision-making authority over different domains, reducing the risk of redundant approvals and bottlenecks. Clearly outlined decision rights streamline accountability and speed up processes.
- **RACI Framework:** Using a RACI (Responsible, Accountable, Consulted, Informed) chart helps clarify the level of involvement each leader has in different decisions or projects.

**Example:** An organization can designate the Chief Marketing Officer as the final authority on brand strategy while making the Chief Digital Officer accountable for all digital channels, with both leaders consulted on overlapping initiatives.

P&G employed the **RACI model** to streamline responsibilities in cross-functional teams when launching a new product. With teams spanning marketing, R&D, supply chain, and customer insights, clarity was essential to avoid delays and ensure accountability. The marketing team handled campaign design and execution. The product manager oversaw end-to-end delivery, made decisions, and owned the final outcome. R&D and consumer research teams were involved for feedback on product testing and branding strategies. Supply chain and sales teams were updated on timelines and deliverables to ensure smooth distribution.

**4. Align Goals to Company Strategy**

- **Unified Leadership Goals:** Ensure all top-level roles align with the company's overarching goals. Establish unified objectives and KPIs to which each leader contributes, fostering a sense of shared responsibility.
- **Cascading Goals:** Allow for role-specific goals that contribute to larger organizational objectives, creating alignment without stifling functional expertise.

**Example:** At Unilever, the Chief Sustainability Officer's goals are directly aligned with the company's ESG objectives, ensuring that sustainability goals resonate across the organization rather than competing with operational targets.

**5. Prioritize Accountability and Performance Tracking**

- **Regular Performance Reviews:** Conduct regular evaluations of each leader's performance, specifically looking at how well they achieve their unique objectives and collaborate with other departments.

- **360-Degree Feedback:** Use feedback from peers and subordinates to assess collaborative effectiveness and identify areas where role overlap may be causing friction.

**Example:** Many companies now use 360-degree feedback for senior executives, allowing them to see how well their contributions align with both team and company goals. Firms like Infosys, ICICI Bank, Wipro, ABG and many others across the globe today use 360-degree assessments.

**6. Consider a Flattened Hierarchy for Certain Roles**

- **Dual-Reporting Structures:** In some cases, flattening the hierarchy can help, especially in roles where close collaboration with different departments is essential. Some organizations have opted for dual-reporting structures for certain positions, where leaders report to more than one senior executive, fostering alignment across functions.
- **Flexible Leadership Teams:** Encourage the creation of project-based leadership teams for high-impact initiatives rather than formal, permanent roles, helping to focus resources on specific projects without inflating the leadership team.

**Example:** Cisco has employed dual reporting structures for its regional leaders, where regional VPs report to both a regional head and a functional head, enhancing cross-functional collaboration.

7. **Invest in Leadership Development and Succession Planning**
   - **Leadership Development Programs:** Offer training and mentorship programs that equip leaders with the skills to navigate complex organizational structures and improve inter-departmental collaboration.
   - **Succession Planning:** Establish a robust succession plan that ensures a smooth transition of leadership roles, helping to prevent redundancy as roles evolve.

**Example:** Companies like Procter & Gamble are known for their rigorous succession planning and leadership development programs, ensuring leaders are well-prepared to collaborate and transition seamlessly as roles change.

By implementing these strategies, organizations can manage the complexity of multiple top positions more effectively, creating a leadership structure that promotes collaboration, reduces redundancy, and aligns with strategic goals.

## Plan for Growth

Ideally, companies can create more capacity through growth. This means going purposefully into new businesses. While this strategy can expand career options, it also assumes that firms pursue unusual or risky opportunities and can appear unprofitable to outsiders and investors. Engaging in this type of growth requires thinking carefully about the costs of hiring someone and providing them with a fulfilling and motivating career. The challenge of career shortages could serve as a catalyst for an established firm to embrace fresh, innovative thinking essential for its growth.

Running a successful organization requires striking the right balance between taking advantage of external opportunities and managing career opportunities. One of the best ways to motivate workers is through career-based incentives. When career opportunities are mismanaged, the firm's performance suffers both in the short run because of career spillovers and intergenerational conflicts and in the long run because such conflicts may make it difficult for the firm to attract new talent. Companies should compare the costs and benefits and not rely on any single approach. An integrative and thoughtful strategy that combines all of these solutions can be the most effective.

## Examples of Organizations with Multiple Top Positions

- **Amazon:** Amazon has multiple executives at the top, including a CEO, COO, CFO, and various specialized roles such as the Senior Vice President of Worldwide Operations and Senior Vice President of North America Consumer. This allows Amazon to maintain its complex logistics and consumer operations at a high level, though it has faced challenges with overlapping functions.

- **Microsoft:** Microsoft has separate leadership roles for technology, customer success, and global operations, supporting its diversified product base. The structure helps the company focus on customer-centricity while driving innovation, though it also adds complexity to cross-functional alignment.
- **Unilever:** With roles like Chief Sustainability Officer, Chief Supply Chain Officer, and Chief Marketing Officer, Unilever can prioritize sustainability and operational excellence in tandem. This structure has made it easier to maintain focus on ESG goals, although it requires strong coordination to avoid role redundancies.

CHAPTER 8

# Innovating from Within: Emergence of Shadow Boards

'Leadership is not about the next election; it's about the next generation.'

– Simon Sinek

## Client Story

A few years ago, in one of my client assignments with a large IT firm, the company we worked with recruited many entry-level engineers and Gen Zs for their consulting division. This recruitment was mainly to support their off-shore centers where they did maintenance and development work of new systems for US and European clients. The recruitment drive of these engineers largely depends on the size and duration of the contract, and it can come and go often depending on business cycles. Therefore, when companies land a large contract, they generally have to ramp up hiring people to fill in the need; and in times, when the contracted work is completed or the pipeline for more work dries up, the excess group of engineers either sit on the 'bench' (a term when engineers wait for their next assignment) or are rotated within the other parts of the organization. How companies use this 'transition' period becomes critical because a long wait with no work can make the new engineer restless and trigger attrition.

Companies in IT consulting roles go all out to attract these employees, doling out many benefits ranging from competitive salaries, working on new technology, a chance to travel and work in different markets, flexible working hours, etc. Despite doing all of this attrition was quite high for the company we worked with. It was higher than the industry average, and they used to lose about 6K of the 10K employees they hired yearly.

For onboarding these engineers, the company used traditional strategies of using recruitment agencies, promoting jobs on company websites, and using popular social media platforms like LinkedIn and so on. It seems every company was doing this, so what was different? Upon several focus groups and informal discussions at different levels the company formed a council of 'Young Gen Zers' who became the task force for revamping the recruitment drive. They formed this group together with insights on what aspiring Gen Zs or young engineers would look for when choosing an employer.

Many things came up, but it was felt one big change needed was to communicate the firm's value proposition to the new employee. The first major change they implemented was having 40 of their top senior leaders create TikTok videos showcasing why people should consider joining the company. They talked about the company values, and culture and why their company was a great choice. Tik-Tok was chosen because it was the one platform where every engineer, they hired was present, and it catered to this generation (content in the form of short and sharp videos). Second, TikTok videos were created for each city where an engineer could be working or posted to help him understand how to navigate during his time in the city. This means there was information on where to stay, the good places to eat, shop, do things over the weekend, nearby tourist spots, and so on. This was done because often young employees had no clue where to begin finding information about the new city, they could be living in. They wanted to make this transition easy. Third, an app was developed specifically for young engineers to apply to the company, offering a streamlined application process that took less than five minutes, eliminating the need to visit the company website. This was done with short attention spans in mind and made it easy, online, and swift.

Finally, within six months of this initiative, a Shadow Board was formed where a council of young and middle engineers were chosen to form the next Vision-Mission statement of this firm. The senior leadership believed a large part of the organization was young and that they should be involved in this exercise as they were the future leaders and should have a voice. Later on, more videos were created where members of this board shared their take on how they see the future of the firm changing with products, offerings they were working on and lastly their own experience of being on 'Shadow Boards.'

Within one year of these efforts, with focused social media campaigns, they saw the recruitment drive becoming easier, attrition reducing, and the employer becoming a preferred choice among young engineers. This initial 'task force', which later became the Shadow Board, was crucial in containing attrition and driving the recruitment strategy of this firm. We will explain how the Shadow Board itself gets formed, but first, what exactly are Shadow Boards? Let's understand what Shadow Boards are and how companies should form them.

## What Is a Shadow Board?

A Shadow Board, sometimes known as a Mirror or Advisory Board, is a secondary group of people to the main board participants, drawn from different backgrounds, not necessarily directors or leaders within the organization, who bring in different perspectives and fresh thinking. This fresh thinking supports organizations in staying relevant. The Shadow Board could contribute to initiatives such as redesigning business models, developing a new marketing plan or updating the organization's value chain. The purpose is to leverage the acumen of younger minds to modify and diversify the insights available to senior executives in the workplace.

This concept of a Shadow Board has been around for some time now. Jack Welch, the famed business leader and former Chief Executive of General Electric (GE), dreamt up the Shadow Board in the early 2000s. He saw it as building on the reverse mentoring system he had developed some years before, which paired senior and junior employees so that the younger ones could teach their older colleagues about technological advances and tools. An effective Shadow Board should offer insight, feedback, and new ideas to senior executives. The members can present their generation's perspective and also learn more about the organization's strategies and decision-making processes. Ideally, everyone benefits.

## The Benefits of a Shadow Board

The main benefits of Shadow Boards are a fresh perspective and a more enthused workforce. Such employee engagement also appears to help corporates keep up to date with market changes and competition. The positive impact of Shadow Boards has been evident before the advent of the COVID-19 pandemic. A recent Harvard Business Review study revealed that organisations that adopted a Shadow Board before the pandemic were better able to respond to the fallout from COVID-19 and the acceleration of digital transformation within the workplace. Ultimately, though, the decision to establish a Shadow Board, and the manner of its establishment, is dependent on the cultural dynamic of a company and the existing management structure.

There are four primary benefits of having a Shadow Board.

**Piloting New Ideas**: The Shadow Board becomes a great way to bounce new initiatives and practices. They can serve as a safe space for the sharing and testing new initiatives at scale.

As we saw from the example at the start of this chapter, piloting ideas with the Shadow Boards allows senior leadership to stay connected to the changing expectations of younger demographics empowering them to pursue bolder strategies.

**Communication**: Organizations seeking to drive workforce engagement – particularly within their younger workers – and improve their ability to respond to changing market conditions may consider implementing a Shadow Board. Such an entity can allow senior executives and rising talent within the organization to communicate with one another, fostering increased understanding at different levels.

**Building Networks, Collaboration and Promotion Prospects**: By having Shadow Boards, the younger employees learn the complexities of the business, see how leaders make decisions and get advice on their goals. The senior leaders get new information and insights from different parts of the company and form personal relationships with rising talent in the pipeline. For the younger and line-level managers, this is a fantastic way to build a network across the firm, which not only helps them to know key leaders but also learn more about the different parts of the business. It is a great way for them to showcase this experience for their onward journey within the firm. In many firms, those selected and worked in Shadow Boards have been fast-tracked with newer opportunities and have risen quickly in the organization ladder.

**Cultural Change**: Finally, Shadow Boards can drive cultural change and digital transformation while inspiring new levels of customer experience as younger employees may represent a closer sample of the organization's customers. These boards can consider harnessing critical skills that may form the future of work (e.g., analytics and data, lateral thinking, design, and creativity).

## How Do Companies Form a Shadow Board?

The motives behind why you want to set up a Shadow Board are key; there is potential for a negative impact if Shadow Boards are not implemented properly. Shadow Boards require genuine commitment from the leadership team to listen to ideas; they need to be prepared to have their assumptions challenged. Excitement and desire for new ideas to be integrated into strategy is essential. Treating the Shadow Board as seriously as setting up a senior leadership team or board of directors is crucial. Proper structure, good governance, clear roles and responsibilities, and proper training are essential. In addition to giving it proper focus, investment of time and resources and commitment to evolution are essential. The most successful Shadow Boards have evolved over time to better meet business needs and unlock potential from new perspectives.

There are five general steps to build and create a working Shadow Board.

**Define Shadow Board Objectives**: It is essential to clearly define the objectives of the Shadow Board. What are you aiming to achieve? Is it being created to foster innovation, bridge generational gaps, enhance digital transformation, or improve sustainability practices? So, for example, if your goal is to understand the views of your youngest consumers and employees, look to Gen Z. But if it is to redesign business models or rethink organizational structure, you can look at Generation X or Millennials. Leaders need to ensure the goals of the Shadow Board align with the company's overall strategic direction.

**Senior Leadership Sponsorship**. Once the objectives have been clearly outlined, it is vital to obtain support from senior leadership to emphasize the importance of the Shadow Board and ensure its recommendations are taken seriously. Once agreed, top leadership needs to communicate the purpose and benefits of the Shadow Board to all levels of the organization.

**Identifying Target Group and Selecting Members:** In order for Shadow Boards to gain traction in the wider organization system, it is crucial to establish criteria for selecting members, such as age (for many, it is typically under 35), diverse backgrounds, roles, and regions within the company. This will bring transparency and trust among all those keen to be part of the Board.

It is important to ensure that the Shadow Board is diverse in terms of gender, ethnicity, function, and geography to bring a wide range of perspectives. Equally important is a discussion about the most prudent way of selecting these members: recommendations from managers or self-nominations from interested employees. If you keep an open application process, it creates more enthusiasm around the Shadow Board. Typically, a more diverse pool of applicants will apply, which helps uncover hidden talent and makes employees feel better represented even if they are not selected.

**Role Clarity of Members and Training:** All members selected in the Shadow Board must familiarize themselves with a charter that outlines the roles and responsibilities. This includes important aspects like the term length for members, which can often be 1-2 years to balance continuity and fresh input. Equally important is for them to know the time commitment. In most organizations, selected members are expected to be on the Shadow Board, in addition to their regular responsibilities, without compensation. So, employees who demonstrate self-discipline to balance both roles are vital. It is also important to have a structure and process. For example, what would be the meeting schedule (e.g., quarterly or bi-annually)? How will the Shadow Board present their ideas to senior executives and receive feedback?

Next, it is also necessary to provide orientation sessions to introduce members to their roles and the company's strategic priorities. Some companies offer training in areas such as strategic thinking, communication, and leadership to enhance their effectiveness.

Finally, it is important to share the successes and contributions of the Shadow Board with the wider organization to build credibility and support while celebrating milestones that the company has achieved with the help of Shadow Boards.

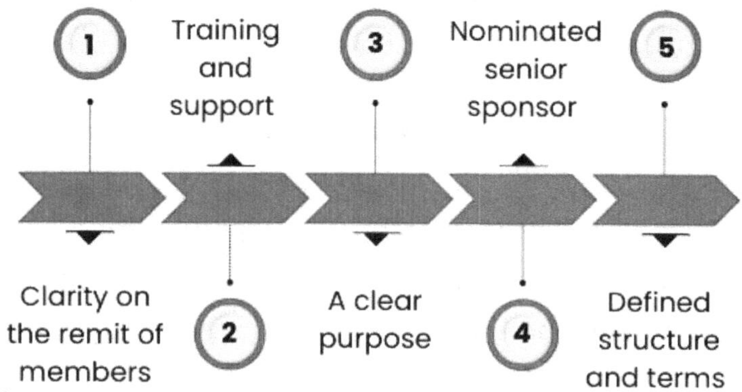


Fig 8.0 Steps in Forming a Shadow Board (@armstrongcraven.com)

## What Are the Downsides of a Shadow Board?

Shadow Boards can bring significant positive changes to an organization provided they are planned and executed well. If not, they can equally present some challenges. There are six main potential pitfalls of a Shadow Board.

**Risk of Group Think:** If the Shadow Board is not diverse enough, there is a risk of Group Think, where members converge on similar ideas and fail to challenge each other effectively. Over time, the Shadow Board may become less innovative if its composition and mandate are not regularly refreshed. Therefore, getting diverse voices and perspectives is essential in bringing new schools of thought and ideas.

**Clarity or Purpose:** Top leadership must clearly define what 'deliverable' is expected of the Shadow Board. In the absence of this, it may just appear that another layer or committee is added to the mix, creating the perception of more bureaucracy and ambiguity in the organization. In one instance, a manufacturing company wanted to find out how young Gen Zers think of a career in manufacturing. Here, it wasn't just enough to ask for their opinions but also to know how the company would use the ideas/recommendations made by the Shadow Board.

**Resistance to Change**: Senior leaders may resist or disregard the Shadow Board's recommendations, especially if they challenge established practices. In one instance, I know a Chief Human Resources Officer (CHRO) had launched and promoted the idea of a Shadow Board, but the CEO saw it as a threat and a distraction. So, if a company has an ingrained culture of resistance to change, it can hinder the Shadow Board's effectiveness and integration.

**Limited Influence**: Shadow Board members may lack the authority to implement their ideas, leading to frustration and disengagement if their contributions are not taken seriously. There is a risk that the Shadow Board may be seen as a token gesture without real impact on strategic decisions.

**Information Sensitivity**: Shadow Board members may be exposed to sensitive or confidential information, requiring strict protocols to ensure data security and confidentiality. It becomes important to ensure effective and secure communication between the Shadow Board and senior leadership.

**Exclusivity Perception and Execution Gaps**: Other employees may feel excluded or undervalued if they perceive the Shadow Board as an elite group with special privileges. The Shadow Board might pursue ideas that, while innovative, are not strategically relevant or feasible given the company's current priorities.

Next is the importance of implementation. Translating the Shadow Board's ideas into actionable strategies can be challenging, especially if there is a lack of support or resources. Participating in a Shadow Board also requires significant time and effort from members, which can detract from their regular job responsibilities. Therefore, it becomes vital for consistent follow-through on recommendations and tracking their impact requires dedicated effort and commitment.

Shadow Boards are a good way to bridge generational barriers and increase trust in the system. It allows for cross-collaboration, blends the generational mix of experience, and opens up new opportunities and solutions. When done rightly, it can help a firm catapult itself to bring innovation from within.

We end the chapter with real examples of companies successfully implementing Shadow Boards.

> Shadow Boards are a good way to bridge generational barriers and increase trust in the system. It allows for cross-collaboration, blends the generational mix of experience, and opens up new opportunities and solutions. When done rightly, it can help a firm catapult itself to bring innovation from within.

**Examples of a Shadow Board**

**Gucci**: In 2015, Gucci was one of the first companies to create a Shadow Board of Millennials, and they have been sharing ideas with each other ever since. These employees addressed strategic oversights and provided a fresh perspective on sales strategies and products. The Chief Executive of the high-end fashion house, Marco Bizzarri, began meeting with the 'shadow committee' of under-30s periodically and credited them with delivering a wake-up call to executives. As a result, Gucci's digital strategies increased sales by 136% between 2015 and 2019. Gucci was also the fastest-growing luxury brand in 2019, and by virtue of this Shadow Board's insight, Gucci was salvaged from its creative coma.

By contrast, the co-CEO of Prada, Patrizio Bertelli, admitted the iconic brand was too slow to respond to digital trends and influencers who were disrupting the fashion industry. The company's sales dropped 11.5% during the same time period.

**Mahindra and Mahindra (India):** Anand Mahindra, Vice-Chairman and Managing Director, wanted to hear the 'voice of the young' not in a casual or ambivalent way but in a serious, structured way. So, in 2003, he added a new circle in the organizational structure to give young managers a voice at the highest levels of decision-making. In 2004, seven promising young managers, all below the age of 35, were hand-picked in each Mahindra company/division and were asked to think of themselves as another management committee. They were asked to choose three to four subjects, anything at all, deliberate on them for two years and make recommendations. Those recommendations might be implemented, junked or filed away, but the assurance was given that the senior management would take them all up. This was Mahindra's initiative of a Shadow Board where young managers would have a voice at the highest level.

Some of the recommendations made by the Mahindra Shadow Boards have found their way into the group's business: the diversification into commercial vehicles, a round-the-clock helpline, a more personal approach to distributing increments, and even a leap into a bold acquisition.

**KPMG**: Professional services firm KPMG implemented a Shadow Board consisting of younger employees, called its 'Millennial Board' which evolved into the next generation council. KPMG reported that the creation of the council resulted in a more robust decision-making process during which traditional norms and views were challenged. KPMG took an active approach, with the council playing a key role in strategic initiatives and offering recommendations and solutions to the executive board. Members of the council also benefited personally through increased visibility, which boosted their career opportunities within the organisation.

**Airbnb** in 2018 revisited a business model and launched a new marketing approach thanks to a Shadow Board.

**Stora Enso** used a Shadow Board to revise how executive members assigned work to employees. The Shadow Board suggested including non-experts in projects to have an unbiased view to increase the chance of a breakthrough. This led to the creation of a new team for a project to reduce lead time in the supply chain. The new team shared a workable plan within a six months' timeframe.

**GroupM India** implemented a three-year digital and cultural transformation. The Shadow Board increased connections between management and low-level employees across agencies through the development of Yammer. The board also strengthened the partnership with media owners, consultants, data providers, auditors and start-ups.

**Accor Hotel** needed a new business model with increased competition from Air BnB. So, the Chief Talent and Culture officer turned to the Shadow Board. Through the Shadow Board, they implemented the concept of Jo & Joe which redefined hostels combining the fun of a hostel and a hotel – an urban shelter which gives creativity, flexibility and a strong sense of community. Accor Pass was also created, a subscription that provided people under 25 with a place to stay while hunting for permanent residence.

**Nestlé** formed a Shadow Board to tap into the insights of Millennials and Gen Z employees, particularly regarding health and wellness trends. The Shadow Board has played a key role in guiding Nestlé's product innovation towards healthier and more sustainable options, aligning with the preferences of younger consumers.

**Unilever's Sustainable Living Advisory Council** helped the company set ambitious sustainability goals, such as reducing greenhouse gas emissions and increasing the use of sustainable packaging. It's also led to more transparent reporting on sustainability performance and engagement with stakeholders on sustainability initiatives.

**Patagonia's Stakeholder Council** has helped the company prioritize sustainable and ethical practices, including using renewable energy, paying employees a living wage, and donating 1% of sales to environmental causes. It's also helped build trust and loyalty with customers who care about these issues.

**Danone's Sustainable Development Council** has helped the company prioritize sustainability in its operations and supply chain. The company has reduced water usage, increased the use of renewable energy, and improved animal welfare in its supply chain. This has helped it win the trust of eco-conscious consumers and build a reputation for sustainability leadership.

**Godrej Group (India)** had a young executive board (YEB) that operated like a Shadow Board and worked closely with the Group Management Committee. While Shadow Boards can be successful if not done carefully, they can fail just as easily. A European Retailer launched a Shadow Board to boost digital innovation but failed due to a misalignment of goals. The Shadow Board focused on strategic recommendations, while leadership needed operational execution. There was also ineffective communication. A lack of transparency in sharing feedback with Shadow Board members diminished their morale. All of this widened the gap between generations, and the program was discontinued after minimal results were achieved.

Shadow Boards work when aligned with specific, actionable goals rather than being a symbolic gesture. Without senior leaders' active support and open-mindedness, Shadow Boards cannot thrive. Establishing how Shadow Boards influence decision-making is critical to avoiding misaligned expectations.

# YOUR GENERATIONAL TOOL KIT

CASES: SCENARIOS

SIMULATING GENERATIONAL ROLES AND CHALLENGES

GENERATIONAL CHEAT SHEETS

UNDERSTANDING I-GEN: YOUR UNDISPUTED 'GEN Z' HUB

# Cases: Scenarios Simulating Generational Roles and Challenges

## 1. Wisdom in Action: Leadership Role of Generations in Shaping Future Leaders

Radha had worked as a support engineer on a systems maintenance assignment upon joining ABC from college. She worked in this role for two years and successfully demonstrated her capability. In this role, her job was to keep the client's system 'UP' without any outages so that they could serve their clients for real-time updates. Responding on time and having strong technical competence are key to the success of this role. Her technical competence and hard work ethic had created a reputation as a reliable team member. Her boss and the client had also been pleased with her support.

After two years in this role, she was ready to try something new within ABC. Her next role was a client-facing (sales) role. Her boss recommended her for this role, and she had finally transitioned to this new role. Sales was new to Radha, and she felt she lacked public speaking or selling skills. After about a week into the role, she had a 1-1 with her boss to understand a bit more about her general background and expectations. In that conversation, she revealed that she can 'NEVER' be a good speaker.

Growing up, she had many A-listers and achievers at home. Her brother Ramesh was always a topper in school and college debates. Her father was a well-published author and was well-known as a thought leader in his field. Seeing her sibling and parents excel, she never felt she had the 'stuff' to be a good orator. Consequently, she always withdrew herself from events or opportunities which required public speaking. Having seen her peers in this role, she was getting a complex of her abilities and rethinking her role as she shared her family background with the boss.

Radha's boss is a Generation Xer. What should the boss do?

**Areas of Discussion:**

- Radha seemed to be demonstrating shades of a fixed mindset (a voice in her mind which is creating limiting behaviors in her ability to do well in people-facing roles due to her family background and upbringing).
- How can the boss explore the origins of this fixed mindset and create a compelling narrative in helping and coaching her on developing a Growth Mindset (being curious about this role on what is possible plus a high try factor to succeed) which will change her perspective and help her succeed in this new role?
- How can an experienced leader from one generation share tips/development needs for a Direct Report/Subordinate of another generation?

## 2. Tech Tensions: Generational Differences in Problem Solving

When Mobio Solutions, a mid-sized tech company, decided to implement a new project management software, the decision-makers quickly realized they were dealing with a classic multi-generational challenge. The Baby Boomers on the team, who had been with the company for decades, were initially skeptical about the new software. Their approach was to rely on tried-and-true methods; they suggested continuing with the legacy systems that had served the company well for years, arguing that the existing tools were familiar and sufficient. They emphasized caution, concerned that a swift transition might disrupt the workflow and cause unnecessary confusion.

On the other hand, the younger employees, particularly the Millennials and Gen Z team members, were enthusiastic about the change. They saw the new software as an opportunity to increase efficiency, streamline communication, and integrate cutting-edge features that would give the company a competitive edge. They proposed a fast-track implementation backed by online tutorials and peer-led training sessions. The tension between the two approaches became evident in meetings, with each generation defending their preferred method. What should the company do?

**Areas of Discussion:**

- Should the company just upskill the Boomer/Xer population explaining the benefits of a new technology?
- Should the company consider delaying the implementation of the new technology based on the feedback from Boomers/Xers? Educate Gen Ys and Zs first on the costs/benefits and a possible deferral in adopting new technology to a future date?
- Create a middle ground by developing a phased rollout plan that combines the Boomers' desire for stability with the younger generation's eagerness to innovate, ensuring a smoother transition for the entire workforce.
- What are some approaches that a company can institutionalize in handling such initiatives in the future that may have generational differences?

## 3. Balancing Priorities: Evolving Work-Life Dynamics across Generations

The leadership team at a global consulting firm faced challenges in establishing a consistent work-life balance policy that satisfied their diverse, multi-generational workforce. The Baby Boomers in the company, who had spent decades climbing the corporate ladder, were accustomed to long hours and often took pride in their strong work ethic. They believed that success required sacrifices, including personal time, and often worked late into the evenings, setting an example for younger employees. To them, the concept of work-life balance was more about managing time efficiently rather than reducing work hours. They advocated for maintaining the firm's high-performance standards, even if it meant occasionally infringing on personal time.

In contrast, the Millennials and Gen Z employees prioritised achieving a healthy work-life balance. They valued flexible work schedules, remote work options, and the ability to disconnect after work hours. For them, work-life balance wasn't just a perk but a necessity for maintaining mental and physical well-being. They pushed for policies that included wellness programs, mental health days, and strict boundaries between work and personal life.

The generational divide became apparent during internal discussions, with younger employees expressing frustration over the expectations set by their older colleagues.

How should the leadership team ultimately navigate these differing perspectives, striving to create a policy that respects the Boomers' dedication while accommodating the younger generation's demand for a balanced lifestyle, which ensures both productivity and employee satisfaction.

## Areas of Discussion

- Should the company encourage and create a culture of longer hours for grooming younger employees to create a strong work ethic when delivering client deliverables? What is the impact of such a practice? Should this be different in the context of a startup?
- How can HR/leaders educate Boomers/Xers and all generations to appreciate the need for mental well-being and the need for work-life balance?
- Does the emphasis on work-life balance come at the cost of productivity?

## 4. Empowering Voices of Generations: Cultivating a Culture of Debate at the Workplace (From Hierarchy to Openness)

Samantha was excited as she stepped into the Synopsis Bangalore office. She had always dreamed of working in India's Silicon Valley city, and she was now there. She has been deputed to be part of the Synopsis Bangalore team from Germany to support an onsite client assignment. She was brought on-site because of her expertise and interest in working with Enterprise Resource Planning (ERP) systems. Her boss in India (Mahesh) was an experienced Synopsite who had led many client engagements over his 15-year illustrious career. He was excited to have Samantha on his team who would bring a new voice and perspective on ERP systems for a crucial implementation for an important client.

There were routine calls for this client between the India team and the client. As is the protocol for this team, Mahesh led the calls (as the senior-most person) and called on his team to get updates and views on specific parts of the project. In one such call during a client discussion, Mahesh recommended a particular approach to implementing the system to the client but Samantha had other ideas/views on going about this. On the same client call she vehemently disagreed with Mahesh and would not back down as she was not logically convinced about his idea. Seeing the banter back and forth between the Synopsis teammates, the client had to step in and request they come to a common agreement to know the right solution.

Upon the conclusion of the meeting, Mahesh was both a bit miffed and unsure of the best way to handle that unplanned confrontation. For him, most of his India teammates normally only spoke when prompted. He knew that it was important to keep the client happy and have them see a unified team. A few hours later, he also reflected to understand Samantha's context and why she was so keen on her way of pushing the solution.

**Areas For Discussion:**

---

- What could be some protocols/SOPs for leading a client meeting when working in a Multi-Gen team?
- What can Mahesh learn about the workplace values and behaviors of the younger generations (especially Gen Y and Zs) when it comes to the expectation of feedback/engagement?
- Similarly, what can Samantha learn about older generations and cultural practices of working in societies and markets like India/Asia?
- How can companies train employees at all levels about the cultural differences within offices of the same organization?

## 5. Climbing Ladders or Exploring Avenues

At a rapidly growing marketing agency, the HR department noticed a significant difference in how employees from different generations approached career development. The Baby Boomers, many of whom were in senior positions, valued traditional career trajectories. They believed in climbing the corporate ladder through hard work, loyalty, and accumulating years of experience. For them, career development meant taking on more responsibilities, mentoring younger colleagues, and eventually moving into executive roles. They preferred structured development programs, like formal leadership training and executive coaching, which aligned with their view of steady, incremental progress.

In contrast, Millennials and Gen Z employees had a more fluid and dynamic approach to career development. They sought rapid advancement, skill diversification, and opportunities for personal growth. They were more likely to explore lateral moves, take on cross-functional projects, or seek roles aligned with their passions. For these younger employees, career development wasn't just about climbing the ladder but about finding meaningful work that offered constant learning and new challenges. They often expressed frustration with the slow pace of traditional career paths and pushed for mentorship programs, online courses, and the freedom to explore unconventional career paths within the company.

How can the leadership balance these contrasting approaches by offering a mix of traditional and modern development opportunities, ensuring that both the seasoned professionals and the younger, ambitious employees feel supported in their career aspirations?

**Areas of Discussion:**

---

- How is the concept of career changing today for employees from different generations? What should companies do to address the differing needs of generations?
- How do employees see careers? Career Ladders versus Career Lattice?

## 6. From Plaques to Praise: Tailoring Recognition in a Diverse Workforce

At a large financial services firm, the Millennials and Gen Z employees had a unique perspective on recognition. They craved immediate and frequent feedback, preferring informal and personalized acknowledgments. For these younger employees, recognition was less about tenure and more about impact and innovation. They valued rewards like flexible work arrangements, opportunities for professional development, and public shout-outs on social media platforms. They also appreciated being recognized for their creativity and problem-solving skills, even if they hadn't been with the company long.

On the other hand, Baby Boomers/Xers, who had been with the company for decades, valued formal recognition tied to tenure and milestones. They appreciated public acknowledgments such as awards ceremonies, plaques, and mentions in company newsletters. For them, loyalty and long-term service were key indicators of success, and they expected rewards that reflected their commitment and contributions over time. The Boomers also valued traditional rewards like bonuses and promotions, viewing them as tangible signs of career advancement.

The management team found themselves navigating these contrasting expectations. They grappled with the challenge of designing a rewards and recognition program that resonated with their multi-generational workforce.

## Areas of Discussion

- How important is designing a good recognition/rewards program in a multi-gen workforce?
- What's a good practice here? Should they ultimately create a hybrid recognition program that honors the long-term dedication of their senior employees while also catering to the younger generation's desire for timely and meaningful acknowledgment?

## 7. Equal Opportunity Leadership: Overcoming Age Bias in Career Development

At a financial services company, concerns over age-related biases in career development began to surface. Older employees increasingly felt overlooked for leadership training and advancement opportunities, with decision-makers often prioritizing younger colleagues deemed more adaptable to modern management trends. Despite their extensive experience and proven track records, senior staff members perceived a growing disconnect between their contributions and opportunities for growth.

On the other hand, younger employees expressed frustration about career stagnation, believing senior colleagues were occupying leadership positions for too long and blocking pathways for upward mobility. These unspoken tensions created a culture of mistrust, where age groups viewed one another as obstacles rather than allies. Resentment began to grow on both sides, threatening workplace harmony and the effectiveness of cross-generational collaboration. How can management address these biases and create equitable opportunities for career development across all generations?

### Areas of Discussion

- How should the company go about looking at the colliding careers among generations?

## 8. Bridging Generational Values: A Shared Vision for Success 'Aligning Values Across Generations'

In a multinational healthcare organization, generational differences in values led to frequent clashes during strategic discussions. Baby Boomers and Gen X employees prioritized stability and long-term patient care programs, viewing these as the backbone of the organization's mission. Meanwhile, Millennials and Gen Z team members pushed for the immediate adoption of innovative technologies, arguing that modern solutions were critical to staying competitive and addressing patient needs in real-time.

The divide became most apparent during budget meetings, where older employees advocated for funding traditional care initiatives while younger employees lobbied for investments in AI and digital tools. Frustration mounted on both sides, with senior staff feeling their decades of experience were undervalued and younger employees perceiving resistance to progress. The lack of alignment slowed decision-making and began to impact the organization's ability to implement timely solutions for patient care. How should management bridge this value gap and ensure collaboration across generations?

### Areas of Discussion

- How can companies balance differing values among generations?

## 9. 'All Voices Matter': Addressing Ageism in Team Innovation

In a fast-paced tech startup, implicit ageism became evident during brainstorming sessions for product innovation. Younger employees, confident in their knowledge of emerging trends and digital tools, often excluded senior colleagues from critical discussions, assuming they lacked the agility or insight to contribute meaningfully. This dynamic left older employees feeling sidelined, undervalued, and reluctant to share their perspectives despite their extensive experience navigating complex challenges.

Over time, the lack of inclusion began to impact team dynamics and innovation. Younger employees missed out on valuable insights rooted in industry expertise, while senior employees disengaged, perceiving little incentive to contribute. The growing divide threatened to undermine the start-up's collaborative culture, which is essential for its success in a competitive market. What steps should management take to address these biases, foster mutual respect, and ensure all voices are heard and valued in the innovation process?

### Areas of Discussion

- How can companies tackle Ageism and Reverse Ageism?
- What would be a good balance which ensures a win-win solution across generations?

# Generational Cheat Sheets: Generational Terminology

**Greatest Generation**: Individuals born between 1901 and 1927. This generation lived through the Great Depression, fought in World War II, and is often praised for its resilience and sacrifice.

**Silent Generation**: Individuals born between 1928 and 1945. This generation experienced the Great Depression and World War II, and is often noted for its traditional values and work ethic.

**Baby Boomers**: Individuals born between 1946 and 1964. This generation grew up during a time of significant social change and economic growth post-World War II.

**Generation X**: Individuals born between 1965 and 1980. Often characterized as being independent, resourceful, and skeptical, this generation experienced the rise of personal computing and the beginning of the digital age.

**Millennials (Generation Y)**: Individuals born between 1981 and 1996. This generation is known for its familiarity with digital technology, social media, and its emphasis on work-life balance and social consciousness.

**Generation Z**: Individuals born between 1997 and 2012. This generation is characterized by its innate use of technology, diverse backgrounds, and progressive views on social issues.

**Generation Alpha**: Individuals born from 2013 onwards. The youngest generation, growing up entirely in the digital age, with access to advanced technology from a very young age. They are often also referred to as the AI generation.

**Generation Beta:** Individuals born from approximately 2025 to 2039, following Gen Alpha. They are expected to grow up in a world shaped by AI, automation, and climate change, with digital integration deeply embedded in their daily lives.

**Xennials**: A micro-generation born between the late 1970s and early 1980s. This cohort bridges the gap between Generation X and Millennials, experiencing both analog and digital childhoods.

**Boomer X:** A transitional micro-generation between Baby Boomers and Gen X which was influenced by both the optimism of Boomers and the skepticism of Gen X. They experienced early exposure to TV, rock music, and shifting societal norms, such as the rise of feminism and changing family structures.

**Zalpha**: A bridge micro-generation between Gen Z and Gen Alpha. They share characteristics of both generations, such as growing up with social media like Gen Z but also starting school in a highly digital environment like GenAlpha. Shaped by the COVID-19 pandemic, their formative experiences reflect a blend of activism and early adoption of virtual learning.

**Digital Natives**: Individuals born or brought up during the age of digital technology, and thus familiar with computers and the internet from an early age. Often used to describe Millennials and Generation Z.

**Digital Immigrants**: Individuals who were born before the widespread adoption of digital technology and have had to adapt to it later in life and are often used to describe Baby Boomers and Generation X.

**Boomerang Generation**: Young adults who return to live with their parents after having lived independently. This term is often used to describe some Millennials and Generation Z members due to economic factors.

**Echo Boomers**: Another term for Millennials, emphasizing their status as the children of Baby Boomers and the 'echo' of the baby boom.

**Sandwich Generation**: Individuals, typically in their 30s or 40s, responsible for bringing up their own children and caring for their aging parents.

**Generation Jones**: Individuals born between 1954 and 1964, at the tail end of the Baby Boomers. This term highlights the cohort's distinct experiences compared to early Baby Boomers.

**Post-Millennials**: Another term for Generation Z, indicating the generation following Millennials.

**iGen**: A term sometimes used to describe Generation Z, emphasizing their integration with technology from an early age.

**Generation C**: A term used to describe a mindset more than an age group, standing for 'connected' generation. These are people who are deeply engaged with digital and social media.

**Generation Flux**: Describes people of any age who thrive in today's era of constant change, characterized by their adaptability and resilience.

**Boomers II**: A sub-group of Baby Boomers, typically those born in the later years of the Baby Boomer generation (1955-1964), who have different experiences than earlier Boomers.

**Tech-Savvy Boomers**: A subset of Baby Boomers who are particularly adept at using technology, often outpacing younger generations in tech adoption and usage.

**War Babies**: Individuals born during World War II (1939-1945), sometimes considered a subset of the Silent Generation.

**Millennial Boomers**: A term used occasionally to describe Baby Boomers who have adopted Millennial characteristics, particularly in their use of technology and social media.

**MTV Generation**: A term often used to describe early Generation X members who were teenagers during the rise of MTV in the 1980s.

**Peter Pan Generation**: Another term for Generation Y/Millennials, emphasizing the tendency to delay traditional adulthood milestones such as marriage and home ownership.

**Generation W**: Occasionally used to refer to women who came of age during the feminist movements of the 1960s and 1970s.

**Lost Generation**: Refers to those who came of age during World War I, typically born between 1883 and 1900. Known for their disillusionment and cultural shifts post-war.

**Generation Zennials**: Another term for Xennials, emphasizing the combination of Gen X's skepticism with Millennials' digital fluency.

**Homeland Generation**: Another term sometimes used for Generation Z, highlighting their post-9/11 upbringing in a homeland security-focused era.

**Millennial X**: A term describing the crossover characteristics between late Generation X members and early Millennials, blending traits from both generations.

**Global Generation**: A term that refers to Generation Z and beyond, emphasizing their global connectivity and awareness due to digital technology.

**Cuspers**: Individuals born on the cusp between two generations, often exhibiting traits from both cohorts. For example, someone born in 1980 might be considered a cusper between Gen X and Millennials.

**G.I. Generation**: Another term for the Greatest Generation, highlighting their participation in World War II and the growth of the American economy post-war.

**Adaptive Generation**: Sometimes used to describe Generation Alpha, emphasizing their adaptability to rapidly changing technologies and environments.

## Generational Stereotypes

### Baby Boomers

1. **Workaholics:** Baby Boomers are sometimes stereotyped as highly dedicated to their careers, often prioritizing work over leisure.
2. **Technological Challengers:** While many Baby Boomers are tech-savvy, there's a stereotype that some struggle with adopting new technologies, leading to jokes about their proficiency with smartphones or social media.
3. **Traditionalists:** Baby Boomers are often seen as valuing traditional institutions and practices, such as hierarchical structures in the workplace or more conservative social norms.
4. **'Back in my day' Mentality:** There's a perception that Baby Boomers tend to reminisce about the past, comparing it favourably to the present and sometimes being resistant to change.
5. **Financially Conservative:** Baby Boomers are often portrayed as financially prudent, prioritizing saving for retirement and being wary of debt.

### Generation Xers

1. **Slackers:** Generation X is sometimes humorously depicted as a cohort of slackers, characterized by their laid-back attitude and scepticism towards traditional career paths.
2. **Latchkey Kids:** Growing up during a time when both parents often worked, Generation X is sometimes ste-

reotyped as being independent and self-reliant from a young age, having spent time alone after school without parental supervision.

3. **Cynical and Sarcastic:** Generation X is often associated with a sarcastic sense of humour and a cynical outlook on life, influenced by the cultural and economic turmoil of their formative years.
4. **Pop Culture Savvy:** Generation X is known for their deep knowledge and nostalgia for 80s and 90s pop culture, including music, movies, and television shows. They may fondly reminisce about cassette tapes, VHS tapes, and iconic TV shows from their youth.
5. **Early Adopters of Technology:** Despite growing up in a pre-digital era, Generation X is often portrayed as being adaptable to technological advancements, embracing the rise of personal computers, video games, and the internet as they came of age.

## Generation Y (Millennials)

1. **Entitled:** Millennials are often stereotyped as entitled and expecting instant gratification, particularly in the workplace, where they may desire rapid career advancement and meaningful work.
2. **Tech-Obsessed:** Millennials are often portrayed as being constantly glued to their smartphones and social media, with a deep dependence on technology for communication, entertainment, and information.

3. **Socially Conscious:** Millennials are often depicted as socially conscious and passionate about causes such as environmental sustainability, social justice, and diversity and inclusion.
4. **Job-Hoppers:** Millennials are sometimes seen as prone to job-hopping, seeking new opportunities and experiences rather than staying loyal to a single employer for an extended period.
5. **Delayed Adulthood:** Due to factors such as economic instability and high student loan debt, Millennials are sometimes portrayed as delaying traditional markers of adulthood, such as homeownership, marriage, and starting a family, in favor of pursuing personal and career fulfilment.

## Generation Z

1. **Tech-Natives:** Generation Z is often characterized as being true digital natives, having grown up with technology and integrated it into every aspect of their lives. They're seen as effortlessly adept at navigating smartphones, social media platforms, and the internet.
2. **Eco-Conscious:** Generation Z is often portrayed as environmentally aware and concerned about issues like climate change, sustainability, and ethical consumption. They may be more inclined to embrace eco-friendly practices and advocate for environmental causes.

3. **Short Attention Spans:** Due to their constant exposure to information and entertainment online, Generation Z is sometimes stereotyped as having shorter attention spans, preferring bite-sized content and quick interactions.
4. **Entrepreneurial Spirit:** Generation Z is often seen as entrepreneurial and resourceful, with a penchant for side hustles, freelance work, and starting their own businesses at a young age. They may be more inclined to pursue unconventional career paths and seek opportunities for self-expression and creativity.
5. **Socially Conscious Activists:** Similar to Millennials, Generation Z is often portrayed as socially conscious and politically engaged, advocating for social justice issues such as racial equality, LGBTQ+ rights, and gun control. They may use their platforms on social media to raise awareness and mobilize for change.

### Generation Alpha

1. **Tech-Savvy from Birth:** Gen Alpha is often seen as the first generation to be fully immersed in technology from day one, with digital devices as an integral part of their daily lives.
2. **Highly Influenced by AI:** Gen Alpha is viewed as being heavily influenced by artificial intelligence, from AI-powered toys to personalized online experiences.

3. **Preference for Visual Learning:** Gen Alpha is thought to prefer visual and interactive learning experiences, relying more on videos and graphics than text-based content.
4. **Overprotected:** Gen Alpha is often seen as the most sheltered generation, with parents and caregivers being hyper-focused on safety and well-being.
5. **Less Independent:** There's a stereotype that Gen Alpha may struggle with independence due to growing up with technology and parents who are more involved in their daily lives.
6. **Demanding Instant Gratification:** Gen Alpha is often described as expecting immediate results and gratification, influenced by the instant access provided by technology and digital services.

## Generational Terminology

**Baby Boomers:**

1. **Groovy:** A term popularized in the 1960s, meaning cool or excellent.
2. **Far Out:** Another 60s term used to express amazement or surprise.
3. **Catch Some Z's:** To get some sleep, referencing the letter 'Z' as slang for sleep.
4. **Sock It to Me:** An expression meaning to give your best effort or to do something well.
5. **Cool Cat:** A term used to describe someone who is fashionable or impressive.
6. **Dig it:** Understand or appreciate something.

**Generation X:**

- **Rad:** Short for radical, meaning cool or awesome.
- **Bling:** Slang for flashy jewellery, often associated with hip-hop culture.
- **As If:** A dismissive phrase, popularized by the movie *Clueless*, expressing disbelief or sarcasm.
- **Chill:** To relax or hang out in a low-key manner.
- **FOMO:** Acronym for 'Fear of Missing Out,' describing the anxiety of missing out on something exciting or interesting.
- **Totally:** 'Completely,' used for emphasis.
- **Dude:** Can refer to anyone; a friendly greeting.
- **Bogus:** Fake or unfair.

**Generation Y (Millennials):**

1. **Yolo:** Acronym for 'You Only Live Once,' used to justify taking risks or seizing opportunities.
2. **Selfie:** A photograph taken of oneself, typically with a smartphone and shared on social media.
3. **Bae:** Term of endearment for a significant other or close friend.
4. **FOMO:** As mentioned earlier, Millennials also commonly use this acronym.
5. **Adulting:** The act of behaving like a responsible adult, particularly when faced with mundane tasks or responsibilities.

**Generation Z:**

- **Slay:** To do something exceptionally well or to dominate a particular activity.
- **Lit:** Used to describe something exciting, excellent, or otherwise impressive.
- **Savage:** Used to describe someone who is fierce, ruthless, or brutally honest.
- **Tea:** Gossip or juicy information about someone or something.
- **Flex:** To show off or boast about one's accomplishments or possessions.

# Understanding i-Gen: Your Undisputed Gen Z Hub

The Gen Z Hub has various sources you can tap into to understand this generation. This is my work done over the last few years.

**Book:** *Target Gen Z*: This is my book on Gen Z which looks at what inspires Gen Z in some of the dimensions such as brands, work-life, learning and others. It is available on Amazon and other major ecom book sites.

**Podcast:** *Working with Gen Z*: This podcast examines all work-related issues as they relate to Gen Z. It is heard in over 60 countries and has now over 50 episodes. You can listen to this podcast on all major platforms: Spotify, Apple, Google, Pod bean and others.

**YouTube Channel:** You will find the video interviews of the podcast

**Ted Talk:** You can listen to my Ted talk on Gen Z called "How can a Gen Z prepare best for future"

**Website:** Here you will find other resources and various talks, I have given on Gen Z as well the interviews I have done as a Gen Z speaker (www.learnwisely.in).

**Social Media Handle**: Here you will see the different postings I have done on Gen Z. https://www.linkedin.com/in/nikhilraval/

Hope you find these resources helpful to understand the Gen Z generation better.

# ALSO, BY NIKHIL RAVAL

Available on Amazon:

https://amzn.to/3t6m2Da https://amzn.to/2OlHwgD

Important Links for You:

Check out the Podcast *Working with Gen Z* available on all major platforms (Spotify, Apple, Google, Pod Bean, Overcast, and others).

**Podcast:** https://podfollow.com/wwgz

**YouTube:** https://www.youtube.com/channel/UCC82LUWJ8Ff_KIVqjVrXCYQ

**Gen Z Ted Talk:** https://www.youtube.com/watch?v=YFdgKrlqgDY

## Some Sprinkling of Talks Delivered on Generation Z

You can catch glimpses of these on www.learnwisely.in or my YouTube Channel

Ahmedabad Book Lovers Club – May 2021

Author Success Stories Podcast – June 2021

IVF - Igniting Mind Series – June 2021

Avanse Financial Services: Managing Leaders of Tomorrow – July 2021

Ted Talk - TEDx JGIS: How to Inspire the Gen Z Generation – Oct 2021

SLASSCOM: Leadership Challenges of Generations in a Hybrid Work Place – January 2022

Indian Society of Training Development (ISTD) – Leading & Engaging Gen Z

Mumbai Chapter: January 2022 / Jaipur Chapter: February 2022 / Noida Chapter – February 2022

National Institute of Design – February 2022

SLASSCOM, Sri Lanka 'How to Lead and Engage Gen Z' – July 2022

Ferrero Group: Leading Change with Generations, Pune – September 2022

Roquette: Collaborate Leadership for Transformative Growth, Nashik – November 2022

TCS: Into Z Future (July 2023), Leading and Engaging Gen Z – June, August, November 2023 / May, June, November 2024, Feb 2025

Astra Zeneca: The Power of One: Lead-Engage-Accelerate-Purpose (LEAP) – February 2023

Computacenter: Lead Inspire Deliver – October 2023

IMS: Skills & Careers for Gen Z – December 2023

General Mills India –Team Alignment & Change – February 2024

HSBC Top 40 DBS Leaders: Leading with Change, Mumbai – March 2024

Conference Board, Singapore: Rising Gen Z – April 2024

Intranet Connections (Vancouver, Canada): Understanding Next Gen Practices – March 2024

91 Spring-Board Talks: Influencing Without Authority for Gen Z – April 2024

IBS Business School: Multi-generational Context @ Workplace – May 2024

Podcast Interview @Gen Z Diplomat: The Reality of Gen Z Workplace Dynamics – May 2024

Podcast Interview@ Powder Coater: Working with People from Planet Gen Z – July 2024

Volkswagen ITS Conference, Managing a Multi-Gen Workforce, Pune – July 2024

Podcast Interview @Mindset Mastery (Money Habits of Gen Z) – August 2024

Max Life Insurance: Leading to Create a Big Picture Mindset – August-September 2024

Veolia / Suez Technologies: Fierce Conversations with Generations – August 2024

Enerpac & Alpha Wave: Fierce Conversations – September and October 2024

Wisdom Meets Innovation: Generational Mosaic – November 2024

Podcast Interview @Sharpen the Spear. Building Gen Z Leaders (Nov, 2024)

Vilfredo Club (BNI) Ahmedabad: Leading a Multi-Gen Workforce – December 2024

Dynamics of a Multi-Gen Workforce. Cutting Edge Program by CEDEP for ABG – Jan 2025

India Diversity Forum – Working with Multi-Gen Workforce – March 2025

# ACKNOWLEDGMENTS

Growing up, I was very lucky to have watched a lot of theater. It came from my father, who was very fond of plays, which also then grew into us with many fond memories. We've seen all genres from comedy to thrillers to those conveying social messages and so on. Contrary to the image one may have about India's booming movie industry (Bollywood), we also have a thriving theater fraternity. Many of the Bollywood actors people admire began their careers as stage actors, and it becomes a great joy to see them in person during plays.

So, when a play ends, the cast normally comes out, and people get to know who they are, and the applause begins. However, after the cast takes a bow, there is also recognition of the 'team' behind the actors who make the play successful. These are the people who are responsible for the costumes, music, lighting, script, dialogues, sound and so on. There is even a louder applause when these members are recognized because what they do behind the curtains as a support, catalyst and anchor makes the whole theater experience come alive. You take any of them out, and the experience is just not the same.

Writing a book is much like the play. There is a cast of people behind the curtain who help the author in his journey to publish a book. The thought of a second book was daunting, but it was the continuous encouragement from my family to do this. Their message to bring to the world the learnings I have seen in my consulting work was compelling. A good book will also help create my brand as an expert in a niche area and as a professional. This included my wife, sister-in-law, brother, the two Gen Z boys (who often joked, *another book, really?*) and everyone in the extended family. Then there were my 'go-to' colleagues who would serve as an honest sounding board on what would make a good topic for the second book, the flow of the book, the logic, the grammar and everything else that goes into writing a full-fledged book. This is everyone from my past colleagues, clients and people I have known in the learning fraternity who gave me honest feedback which was crucial in shaping the manuscript and its flow. John Malitoris, Sandhya Karpe, Cindy Campbell, Eliza Quek are some of these colleagues. I also thank all my former clients and colleagues who were willing to pen a line of praise after reading the edited version. Third is the publishing team at Happy Publishing, who helped me begin my journey as an author. Their efficient and able team was helpful in editing, proofreading, and designing which made this book come alive. This is Jyotsana, Sunaina, and Sushmitha.

But perhaps the most important of all stakeholders are the YOU (the readers), who encouraged me to continue to write based on the success and sales of my first book. An author's journey can often be lonely without the reader's acknowledgement. The support I have received in the forms of messages, my podcast, and invites to speaking engagements made me feel more convinced that the topics I have chosen have a need for someone. Even if I can make a small impact on a group of a multi-generational team somewhere, it will all be worth it.

# ABOUT THE AUTHOR

Nikhil Raval is a leadership, learning, and change-OD expert who passionately believes the role of learning in its many forms is to lift the societies it serves. He believes that organizations that we work for also have the responsibility to serve society. At the intersection of these two forces lies leadership development, a pivotal element in driving meaningful change. Whether it's a fresh graduate entering the workforce or a seasoned professional adapting to an evolving world, every effort to help a leader improve not only enhances their life but also positively impacts the lives of their team members, strengthens their organization, and contributes to the betterment of society as a whole.

After a successful career in Financial Services for nearly a decade in the US, he forayed into Leadership Consulting and led as the MD and Board Member of Duke CE, India. He is the author of the bestselling book *Target Gen Z: Understanding the Gen Z Mindset on Brands, Work-Life, Learning and More* released in 2021. He is also the host of the popular podcast *Working with Gen Z* which examines all facets of the Gen Z generation at the workplace, heard over more than 60 countries. His work has taken him to more than 30+ countries. A multiple-time TED speaker and award-winning presenter, he continues to inspire leaders at every stage of their journey.

www.learnwisely.in

# THANK YOU

Thank You For Reading My Book!

I really appreciate all of your feedback, and I love hearing what you have to say.

I need your input to make the next version of this book and my future books even better.

Please leave me a helpful review on Amazon letting me know what you thought of the book.

Thank you so much!
Nikhil Raval

9 789334 284980

Printed at Repro India Ltd.